PUCCINI

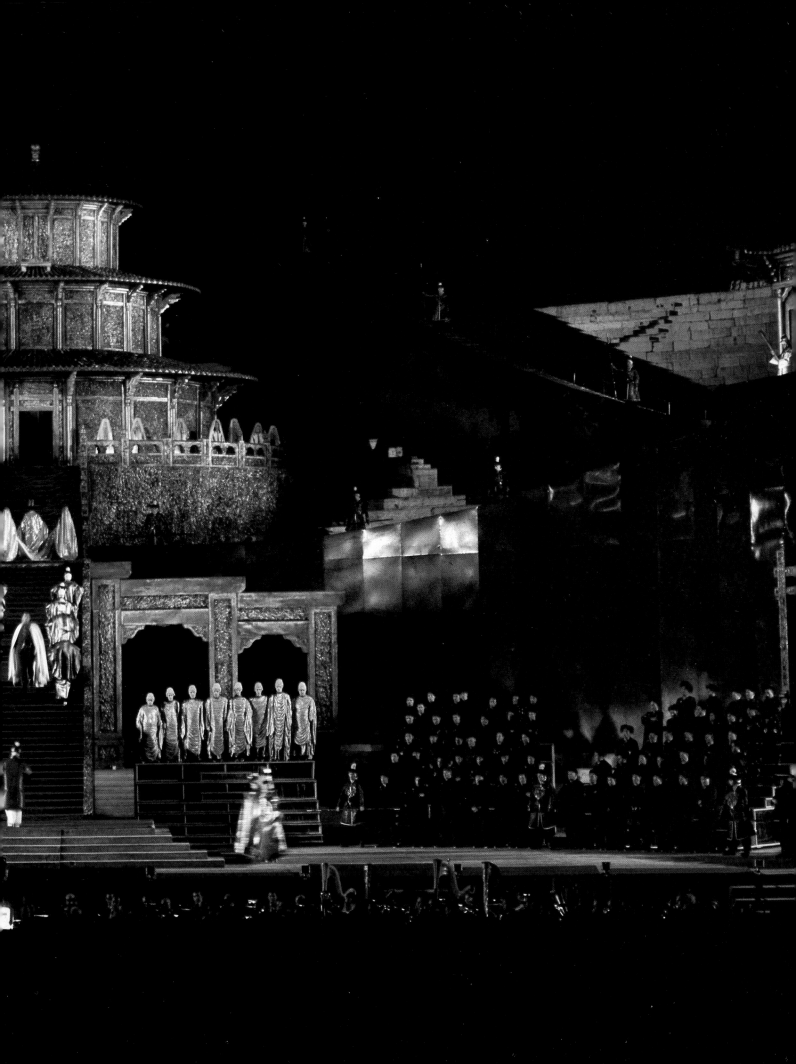

On the cover:
PUCCINI, portrait by Arturo Rietti (1863-1943)
Milan, Museum of La Scala Theater

Text by Giuseppe Tarozzi

Edited and translated by John W. Freeman
Chapter: ''Puccini in America'' by Mary Jane Phillips Matz
Epilogue: ''Puccini the Artist'' by John W. Freeman

Published by Treves Publishing Company; a Division of
Elite Publishing Corporation
120 East 56th Street
New York, New York 10022

Library of Congress Catalog Card Number: 85-5861.
ISBN: 0-918367-06-9

PORTRAITS OF GREATNESS
(Service Mark Application Pending)

Printed and bound in Italy by Officine Grafiche
Arnoldo Mondadori Editore, Milano, Italy, April 19, 1985

End papers:
Scene from *Turandot*
staged at Verona Arena, 1969,
direction by Luigi Squarzina,
set design by Pier Luigi Pizzi

Facing page:
Detail of monument to Puccini
that stands in front of
his villa at Torre del Lago

PORTRAITS OF GREATNESS

PUCCINI

by Giuseppe Tarozzi

translated by John W. Freeman

**TREVES
PUBLISHING
COMPANY**

Below, a portrait of the first Giacomo Puccini (1712-81), the composer's great-great grandfather, a noted organist of the eighteenth century. By family right the Puccinis were court musicians and organists of the Cathedral. The portrait hangs today in Lucca.

Next to him, the composer's grandmother, Angela (née Piccinini), wife of Domenico. Below, the composer's parents, the former Albina Magi, a major force in young Giacomo's life, and Michele, himself a composer, who died when the boy was five.

Celle, in the Val di Roggio in the Province of Lucca, is a small, rather hilly countryside, rising a few kilometers from Pescaglia. Around there the earth is reddish, spotted with the greenish silver of oliver trees, with groves of larches and oak. The sky is lofty, very often clear; and beyond this polished blue mirror, there in the distance, in an almost imaginery line, one senses the ocean.

It was right here, in this cluster of houses spread across the gentle corner of Tuscany that is already blending into Liguria, that the Puccini family had its beginnings. The first of the Puccinis of whom we know anything for sure is one Giacomo (whose name would remain a family tradition), who lived in the 1700s, was in touch with Padre Martini—a noted composer of the period—and who was both a good organist and a fair composer. It is apparent that the vocation of music was, so to speak, inherited, passing from those distant eighteenth-century beginnings through the branches of the family tree to those various Puccinis who were born, worked and died there. Among them, at least Domenico (1771-1813) and Michele (1812-1864), father of the composer of *La Bohème,* should be mentioned. Domenico was a pupil of Paisiello in Naples and wrote concertos and cantatas of merit. Michele in his turn, a mild, reserved man, perhaps also frustrated in hopes grander than his abilities, studied for a time with Mercadante and Donizetti, in the course of a sojourn in Naples. Returning to Lucca, he took the post of choirmaster and organist in the Cathedral. He wrote two operas, two masses with orchestra, a Miserere, some antiphons. For the most part, he wrote his music for special occasions, showing noteworthy technical skill and a sound gift for melody. He died rather young, not well off financially and the father of seven, six of them girls—Odilia, Tomaide, Iginia, Nitteti, Romelde, Macrina—and one a boy, Giacomo. His wife, when widowed, was pregnant with one more son, Michele, born six months after his father's death.

Giacomo, who was five years old, and who would keep elusive memories of his father, inherited from him the post of organist, choirmaster and superintendant of music at St. Martin's, all titles that by acquired right belonged to the eldest male child of the Puccini clan.

Left, document of the Puccini family, among the records of the municipality of Lucca. Below left, the Puccinis' house in Celle, a hill town near Pescaglia, before the family left in the eighteenth century to make their home in Lucca. Below right, the family crest.

5

Upper left, a view of Lucca in the 1700s, when it held fewer than 40,000 inhabitants and was independent of the Grand Duchy of Tuscany. To the right, the tower that surmounts the Guinigi Palace, one of the landmarks identified with the city. Below, the surrounding walls, which remain a favorite walking place for the people of Lucca. These walls extend more than four kilometers, shaded by a wealth of trees. Within these confines Lucca preserves intact its inimitable face and some of the most beautiful monuments of Italian history: paintings by Ghirlandaio, Tintoretto, Fra' Bartolomeo and especially the tomb of Ilario del Carretto, the work of Jacopo Della Quercia, unsurpassed in its genre.

II. LUCCA

The house of the Puccinis in Lucca. Above, the main hall, with its promenade and ancestral portraits. The Puccinis were not wealthy, but they had to keep up appearances befitting their hereditary status as court musicians. Giacomo learned to endure the pain of this decorous poverty, which was the common lot of Italy's petite bourgeoisie. Below,

the exterior of the house, a few steps from the awesome Cathedral Square and not far from the Conservatory. Puccini never had the happiest recollections of his hometown, moving away as soon as he could, going to live first at Torre del Lago, later at Viareggio when industrialization began to erode the rural privacy of Torre del Lago.

An enchanted city, straight out of a storybook, Lucca was founded by the Ligurians, who were succeeded in history by the Etruscans. Then came Roman rule, and the little town was bounded by walls that would last through the thirteenth century. During that period, as it developed into a city, strong in a spirit of communal independence, Lucca saw fit to deploy the encirclement of walls for some four kilometers. Within this boundary, the town grew rich and beautified itself with piazzas, monuments, palaces, wide-open spaces and narrow ones. The coast is not far off; to the north rise the Apuan Alps, from there the Appenines of Pistoia; to the west the countryside rolls away gently.

Up through the first half of the next century, Lucca was independent of Tuscany, and if the accent, the language, was Tuscan, the character of the people was rather different—milder, less aggressive and sharp, a bit contrary, proud of their own history and their own peculiarities.

When Giacomo Puccini was born, on December 22, 1858, Lucca boasted some 40,000 inhabitants, an oval marketplace (which happily remains today), a Cathedral—St. Martin's—a city theater and dozens of palaces, of which the most important and beautiful was (and still is) the Palazzo Guinigi, a geometric structure of clean, clear lines, with shafts rising to the tower, where architectural soundness is wedded with something of the happily absurd. In this city a life goes on that is calm, sheltered, provincial, still regulated by the course of the seasons. A city conservative to the core, attached to traditions that have the status of law, rich in monuments and art treasures among Italy's finest. It is worth the trouble to single out the baptismal font of the Church of San Frediano (from the twelfth century); that of St. Michael in Faro (from the fourteenth), with its stunning façade and paintings by Ghirlandaio, Fra' Bartolomeo, Tintoretto and, above all, the tomb of Ilario del Carretto, the work of Giacopo Della Quercia (1408), one of the most celebrated of its kind.

The beauty of Lucca, evident in its agricultural origins, is modest, rather hidden from the hurried visitor. It is a city to be discovered little by little, to come to love lastingly. Such were the early surroundings of Giacomo Puccini.

The Church of San Paolino was frequented by the good burghers of Lucca, who were devout and conservative, much attached to religious ritual and sung masses, obedient to the instructions of the local curia and its ministers. At San Paolino, young Giacomo Puccini regularly displayed his talents as a budding organist.

Bottom left, the façade of the church; at right, the organ on which Puccini, little more than a boy, played during religious services. This was one of several ways open to him for augmenting his meager income, so he could have a few coins of his own in his pocket; the Church of San Paolino was not the only showcase for his talents.

III. FIRST STUDIES

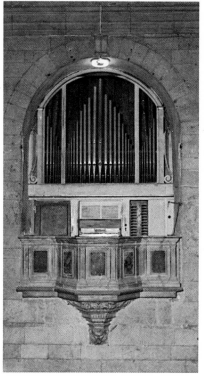

Elementary school, grammar lessons, arithmetic, history, geography. But above all the study of music. If he were to become superintendent of music when he came of age, Giacomo had to begin preparing right away. This was Puccini's boyhood. At home there was little money, and the mouths to feed were many. No poverty is quite so hard to bear, from a psychological viewpoint, as that which strikes those belonging to the petite bourgeoisie. It is necessary to make sacrifices and maintain dignity. Perhaps some of Puccini's complexes were born here.

At first, Giacomo did not seem a child especially gifted for music. He was easily bored, often absent or absent-minded, and did not make notable progress. Rather than pursue notes and scales, he seemed inclined to go hunting for birds' nests, to break away to play on the ancient walls of Lucca, to get into mischief. In the last year of high school, he failed. His musical apprenticeship had begun under the guidance of a strict but good-hearted uncle, Fortunato Magi. Two years went by, and the uncle pronounced his first judgment: this Puccini seemed likely to be the exception that proved the rule. He had neither the ear nor the aptitude nor the calling of a musician. Giacomo changed teachers and was placed under the tutelage of Maestro Carlo Angeloni, a former pupil of the boy's father. Another young man of Lucca who was studying with Angeloni, older and more advanced than Giacomo and very well spoken of, was Alfredo Catalani.

Under Angeloni, Puccini made progress, so much so as to earn his first fees, both giving lessons to children and presenting himself as organist in the churches of the countryside around Lucca, or entertaining clients at a house of pleasure by playing the piano. By now he had grown into a tall boy, not yet knowing with any exactitude what his future would be, or in what dreams to place his trust. If he did know, he told nobody. One thing, however, he knew with stubborn determination: he wanted to get rich. He was tired of leading the life of an orphan, subsisting on town welfare and donations, unable to live like many others his age, suffering the cold of winter because he needed to save up for wood to light the fire. He wanted to be rich, free and independent. He wanted to assert himself and redeem himself.

Left, one of Lucca's old streets, dark and narrow. In streets like this were found "houses of pleasure," and in these too the young student Giacomo Puccini was to be found. There was always an upright piano, on which Puccini played songs and dances for the habitúes—another means by which he could try to balance his always precarious budget.

Above, Giacomo Puccini as a student at the Conservatory. Lower left, the courtyard of the Conservatory of the City of Lucca. At first Giacomo was not an outstanding student. He showed himself to be lazy and self-willed, with little interest in composition. As the years went by, however, his attitude toward music gradually emerged. He admired a fellow student, Alfredo Catalani, who was older and more advanced— the future composer of La Wally. *Puccini began to study with motivation: he understood that his future, his chance to get ahead in the struggle of life, lay in the direction of becoming a composer of music that would appeal to the public. In Italy, this meant music for the church or for the theater—specifically the opera theater.*

Below, title page for the study score of Verdi's latest opera, Aida, written to solemnize the opening of the Suez Canal. Puccini made a trip to see this opera, and it galvanized his determination to pursue a career as an opera composer, inspired by Verdi's example and following in the celebrated old man's footsteps.

Right, announcement published in an Italian journal about the death of Victor Emmanuel II, known as "the gentleman king." Lower right, Giuseppe Verdi conducting the Italian premiere of Aida in 1876. The veteran of Sant' Agata made podium appearances less and less often; his last was to lead his Messa da Requiem *in memory of Manzoni.*

L'ILLUSTRAZIONE ITALIANA

Pur troppo le speranze nostre e dell'Italia furono deluse. Al momento di mettere in macchina ci giunge la notizia che il primo Re d'Italia non è più! Dopo soli cinque giorni di malattia.

VITTORIO EMANUELE II

morì mercoledì 9 gennaio alle 2 1⁄2 pom. fra i conforti della religione e il lutto della nazione. Sì! il lutto è grande, sincero, in tutte le città e i borghi d'Italia. Ad ogni famiglia pare d'aver perduto uno dei suoi cari. I contemporanei gli avean dato il nome di RE GALANTUOMO; i posteri confermandogli questo titolo sì ben meritato aggiungeranno ch'egli fondò l'Italia. Possa il suo figlio UMBERTO I che oggi sale sul trono emulare le sue virtù e meritarsi la sua popolarità. È il miglior augurio che dal cuore addolorato per un sì grande disastro nazionale possiam fare alla patria!

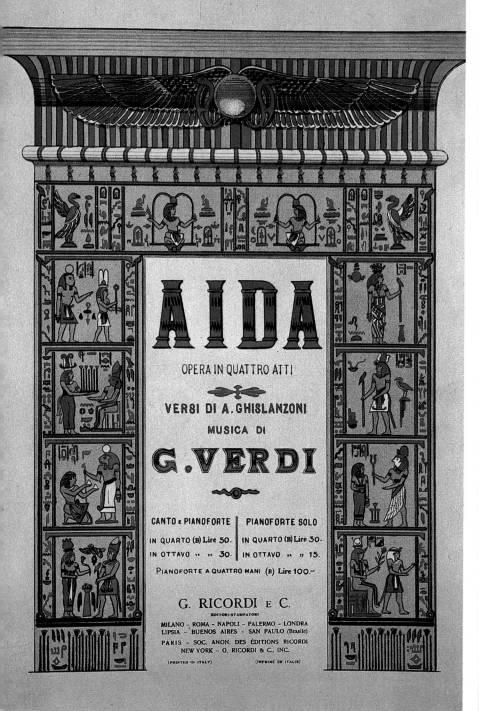

AIDA

OPERA IN QUATTRO ATTI

VERSI DI A. GHISLANZONI

MUSICA DI

G. VERDI

CANTO E PIANOFORTE	PIANOFORTE SOLO
IN QUARTO (B) Lire 50.	IN QUARTO (B) Lire 30.
IN OTTAVO ,, ,, 30.	IN OTTAVO ,, ,, 15.
PIANOFORTE A QUATTRO MANI (B) Lire 100.—	

G. RICORDI E C.
EDITORI-STAMPATORI

MILANO – ROMA – NAPOLI – PALERMO – LONDRA
LIPSIA – BUENOS AIRES – SAN PAULO (Brasile)
PARIS – SOC. ANON. DES ÉDITIONS RICORDI
NEW YORK – G. RICORDI & C., INC.

(PRINTED IN ITALY)   (IMPRIMÉ EN ITALIE)

IV. TO PISA FOR "AIDA"

He was not yet eighteen when he tempted fate: he entered a competition announced by the community for a musical composition paying tribute to the recent death of the father of the country, King Victor Emmanuel II. Giacomo Puccini wrote his hymn and submitted it to the board of judges. The outcome was not very promising. The hymn failed, and the president of the committee accompanied his negative vote with an exhortation to the young composer to apply himself more to musical technique, studying it with great seriousness.

This sudden setback did not faze Puccini. He had arrived at a decision that nothing could make him withdraw: his future would be music, his source of livelihood would be notes. This flash of lightning on the road to Damascus, as the artist would recall when he became world famous, struck one calm night toward the end of winter, between March 11 and 12, 1876. Performances in Pisa had been announced for Giuseppe Verdi's most recent masterpiece, *Aida*. As usual, Puccini had little money—just enough to pay for admission. Not losing heart, he traveled on foot the thirty-odd kilometers that separated the two cities. Hearing *Aida* won him over and made up his mind. On the way home, in the middle of the night, he determined to be the future claimant to the heritage of Verdi.

He immersed himself in his studies with renewed diligence. In that same year, 1876, he wrote his Symphonic Prelude, and two years later a Motet and a Credo that were performed in Lucca, garnering his first favorable notices. By now, however, he was starting to feel confined by Lucca. The job of director of the local music school no longer interested him, and neither did that of church music director. He wanted to aim higher, and he had already learned everything Lucca had to teach him. He needed a real conservatory, broader cultural horizons, real teachers. So his mother wrote to Queen Margherita, beseeching her to "come to the aid of a young man desirous of making a way for himself." After quite a long wait, the request was granted: Giacomo Puccini would receive 100 lire per month for one year. He could go to Milan to try his fortune. It was in Milan that an aspiring musician could get the best education and the best opportunities.

Upper picture: the Milan Conservatory, then as now one of the most important in Italy. As a young man, Verdi had applied there and been rejected—a slight he never forgave—as being over the age limit and not sufficiently skilled in music. Puccini on the other hand was an excellent student, promoted by his teacher Ponchielli.

Below, The Hour of Repose, *painting by Filippo Carcano. Toward the end of the nineteenth century, Milan was a very lively city, Italy's most advanced in business and economic affairs. It was also the publishing capital for papers, books and magazines. In Milan the first socialist groups and workers' mutual-aid societies appeared.*

V. AT THE MILAN CONSERVATORY

Toward the middle of October 1880, Giacomo Puccini, holding a diploma from the Pacini Institute of Music in Lucca, armed with a study grant authorized by Queen Margherita, arrived in Milan to enroll at the Conservatory. Fall was in the air—dark and cold, with frequent rain. The city, overcast with gray, was full of traffic, crowds and confusion. It was hard to form a first impression. Puccini felt rather drawn to Milan and, at the same time, repulsed by it. He stayed at No. 2, Vicolo S. Carlo (St. Charles Lane), where, as he wrote to his mother, he had "a nice little room, very clean, with a handsome polished-walnut desk that is a thing of beauty." November soon arrived, and with it the time to take the entrance examination. This is what he said in another letter: "I have very serious hopes of being accepted, because I've gotten good grades . . . My exam was a bit of foolishness, because I was asked to fill out the accompaniment to a single line of music, without figured bass and extremely easy. Then they had me improvise on a D-major melody that turned out not to amount to much; that's all, and it went well."

The result justified his hopes: our candidate won first place. And so it was that on December 7 he started lessons. He applied himself without losing any time, keeping his eye on the essential thing—to become a master of technique. He set himself a schedule and stuck to its scrupulously. This is what he wrote in a letter: "In the morning I get up at 8:30. When I have a lesson, I go to it: otherwise I practice piano for a while. I just bought an excellent practice book by Angeleri, one of those methods that let you teach yourself, very good. At one o'clock I'm back at the house, studying for Bazzini [director of the Conservatory] for a couple of hours. Then, from three to five, off again at the piano, and a little reading of classical music . . . At five I go for a modest repast (emphasis on the 'modest') and eat some Milanese minestrone, which is pretty good, to tell the truth. I have three plates of that, then something else to fill me up—a little piece of cheese with *bei* and a half-liter of wine. Afterward I light up a cigar and go for a stroll in the Galleria, back and forth, as usual. I'm there till nine and go home all walked out. Back at my room I do a little counterpoint, then go to bed and read a few pages of a novel. That's my life."

Milan's central station, above, was already, at the end of the nineteenth century, a point of arrival for many immigrants. They came especially from poor sections of Puglie and the Veneto. Milan was also the site of arrival for many intellectuals, ready to try their luck among the many activities the city had to offer. Milan was a pulsing, producing city, alive with the spirit of initiative. It was also the center of Italy's musical life and, as such, the capital of the world empire of Italian opera, ruled by Milan's influential music publishers. Below, a horse-drawn tram on one of Milan's broad streets, showing the metropolis as Puccini knew it, with its solid, monumental style of architecture.

Below, La Scala, the most famous opera house of Italy—and the world. There the success or failure of a composer was decided. Its opera season was the most ambitious in Italy, and the most closely watched. Middle pictures: Marco Praga (left) and Giovanni Rovani, writers and playwrights both, enjoyed good success. Bottom left, Biffi's Restaurant.

Right, a view of Via Dante during the second half of the nineteenth century, one of the nerve centers of Milan. Below it, portrait of Giuseppe Verdi painted in Paris by Giovanni Boldini. Verdi was the patron saint of Italian music. Giulio Ricordi knew how to make the most of the public's anticipation of the Maestro's rare premieres.

VI. THE CULTURAL LIFE OF MILAN

Milanese culture expressed itself in scapigliatura *(Bohemianism), modeled on the French avant-garde, reacting against classicism and tradition. Among the Bohemians were Rovani, Arrigo Boito and Cleto Arrighi (top row). Their goal was expression free of preconceived schemes, based on feeling. Their* bêtes noires *were Carducci and Manzoni.*

Center, the two great Milanese publishers Sonzogno (Ricordi's rival in the music field) and Treves, who published D'Annunzio. Bottom, a caricature representing musical Bohemians, the "young school," fostered especially by Sonzogno: left to right, Pietro Mascagni, Ruggero Leoncavallo, Giacomo Puccini and Alberto Franchetti.

At the end of the last century, Milan was a city already at the avant-garde in Italy. Business, industry and artisanship flowered there. It was the financial capital of Italy, guided by a very solid, pragmatic bourgeoisie that wanted to be up and doing, to make an impression, to become the city's dominant class. Musically too, Milan was the richest city in the country. Above all there was La Scala—the leading opera house of the world, the theater that could make or break a composer. And there was the Conservatory, one of the strictest: Giuseppe Verdi himself had not been accepted there, because of its stingy musical attitudes. Otherwise there flourished a variety of concerts and chamber music enterprises. Not long before, a daily paper had been born, *Il Corriere della Sera* (The Evening Courier), which was already on its way to becoming the most authoritative and widely circulated in the entire nation. There were other papers too, like *La Perseveranza* (The Go-Getter) and *Il Secolo* (The Century), which formed opinion and had their share of followers. There were publishing houses—Sperling & Kupfer, Treves—and only in Milan were there music publishers to rank with those abroad—Ricordi, Sonzogno, Lucca.

Aside from official culture, that which still gathered around the memory of Alessandro Manzoni, Italy's greatest nineteenth-century novelist, in Milan in those years there took hold a movement that would reach out into other parts of Italy, especially the Piedmont—bohemianism, called *scapigliatura* (dishevelment, hippie-ism) by the Italians. Born of romanticism, drawn by the French experiments of Baudelaire and the *poètes maudits* (cursed poets), bohemianism aimed to rebel against the courtly forms of art, then personified by Carducci, and to make itself over according to free inspiration and imagination. There were bohemian poets like Arrigo Boito and Marco Praga, bohemian writers like Eugenio Rovani. Alongside the bohemians, the verists too began to press forward, hoping to show life as it actually was. Giovanni Verga, Italy's major verist, began his experiments right in Milan. The movement called *verismo* (verism, realism) also drew a following among young composers—Ruggero Leoncavallo, Pietro Mascagni. Puccini, at least at first, was a verist too.

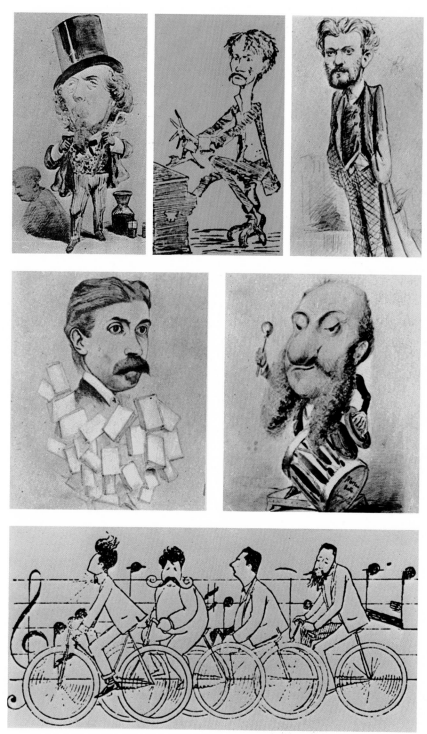

*Amilcare Ponchielli from Cremona, successful composer, teacher at the Milan Conservatory. He was a kind, courteous, mild-mannered man. As a musician he was able to win a minor place in history as an epigone of Verdi. Ponchielli stood at a difficult crossroads in the evolution of Italian opera. Verdi was still searching out new paths (*Aida, Otello, Falstaff*),*

but his followers stuck to the safer ways of his great successes, reducing their characters to mere formulas, looking for sure-fire effects. Among these followers Ponchielli held a respectable place: his best-known work, La Gioconda, *is redeemed by an elegiac lyricism that bore praiseworthy musical fruit, showing a ready melodic inspiration.*

VII. PONCHIELLI'S PUPIL

Puccini readily earned the good will of his teachers. He was diligent, attentive, prepared his work carefully and learned quickly. For the rest, he knew he had no other way to get ahead than through his own talent and intelligence. For him there were no other choices: either he was to become a composer well-liked by the public, or he would have to resign himself to a quiet, mediocre life as a music teacher. The first to take notice of him was the director of the school, Antonio Bazzini, who urged him to keep at it and apply himself. He further did him the honor of inviting him to his home, so that his name began to circulate in musical circles, among the publishers. But the one who really assured him a proper reputation, who pointed him out to the various Ricordis and Sonzognos, was Amilcare Ponchielli, his composition teacher. A quiet man from Cremona, his face adorned with a huge beard, and a hearty eater, Ponchielli was a successful opera composer himself. Following the example of Verdi without achieving the same greatness, he had written several operas, among them *I Promessi Sposi* (based on Manzoni's most famous novel), but he owed his fame to *La Gioconda,* a four-act melodrama given for the first time at La Scala in April 1876, to a libretto by "Tobia Gorrio" (anagrammatic pseudonym of Arrigo Boito), based on the play *Angelo, Tyrant of Padua* by Victor Hugo. It had earned a triumph and gone the rounds of all the theaters for some fifty productions. Ponchielli took a liking to Puccini, and he too invited him to his home.

Writing to the mother of the young man from Lucca, Ponchielli expressed himself this way: "Your son Giacomo is one of the best pupils in my class, and I am well pleased with him. I would say '*very* well pleased' if he would apply himself a little more assiduously, since when he feels like it, he does so well. Giacomo, over and above what he has to do for school, should busy himself seriously with his art and *write*—write, turn out music."

Frequently Ponchielli's home, Puccini got to know the men and women who counted in his world: Signora Giovannina Lucca, Wagner's first Italian publisher; Arrigo Boito; the celebrated conductor and symphonic composer Giuseppe Martucci. He didn't talk much. Instead, he listened and learned.

Left, a cariacature of Amilcare
Ponchielli. Below, librettos
for three of his operas, all
produced at La Scala. Marion
Delorme, *his last opera, dates
from 1885. For a certain time
Giovanni Ricordi, Italy's greatest
music publisher, fixed his
attention on Ponchielli, but after
a while the composer's promise
went no farther.*

Top picture below: Arrigo Boito,
*writer, poet, journalist, librettist,
himself a composer (*Mefistofele,
Nerone*), leading figure in
Milan's cultural life. After
having once taken exception
to Verdi, he put himself at the
older man's service as librettist
for* Otello *and* Falstaff. *Bottom,
three great Milanese periodicals,
including Ricordi's* Gazzetta.

VIII. FOUR STEPS IN THE GALLERIA

Two pictures of Giacomo Puccini in Milan: as young Bohemian (directly below), when he was still relatively unknown and writing Le Villi, and in the Galleria after La Bohème (bottom), when he had achieved world fame. The Galleria was a rendezvous point for successful and aspiring people from every field of endeavor, a kind of social club for all Milan.

The Galleria Vittorio Emmanuele, just to one side of the Milan Cathedral, uniting the latter's open square with that of the Teatro alla Scala, was—then as now—the main lobby of Milan. There at the required times, half past noon and 8:30 in the evening, everyone passed through. There one could find, regardless of the season, as if by prearranged appointment, the big names of the city—those of finance and industry, the intellectuals and artists. The main office of *Il Corriere della Sera* was in the Galleria. There too was the Café Stoker, which later became the famous Savini Restaurant. The Stoker was a hangout for bohemians. Puccini would saunter past, smoking his Tuscan *mezzo,* casting a curious eye to pick out Arrigo Boito or Marco Praga or perhaps Ruggero Leoncavallo, who still hadn't decided whether to devote himself to journalism, poetry or opera composition. In the meantime, Leoncavallo was making himself known. There too was the music publisher Giulio Ricordi, who came in the company of an old gentleman, dressed in black like a country squire, his face chiseled, his beard white—Giuseppe Verdi. And there were Giuseppe Rovani, Giovanni Verga, Gerolamo Rovetta.

Among those frequenting the Galleria was a fortyish man, his face suggesting D'Artagnan of *The Three Musketeers,* his words always forceful, inclined toward polemics—Luigi Illica, already a known librettist, a theater man of rare gifts and a versifier of fantasy if not always the greatest refinement. Another sometimes to be found at the Stoker was Giuseppe Giacosa, a placid, fat man already famous for two plays that had achieved noteworthy success—*Tristi Amori, Come le Foglie* (Sad Loves, Like the Leaves) and *La Partita a Scacchi* (The Chess Game). He had written poetry, full of rather mannered decadence but stylish and able, and he was one of the prestigious writers for *Il Corriere della Sera.*

So back and forth went Puccini in the Galleria. He would stop for coffee, trying not to drink much, because he was always short of cash and had to watch his expenditures carefully. He was dreaming, hoping, waiting. Sooner or later, his big chance would arrive. One needed only to be quick enough not to let it get away. He had been taught from childhood that fortune never knocks a second time.

Cultural life in particular centered on the Galleria (below); in an idealized group portrait (left) appear Mascagni, Puccini, leoncavallo, Catalani, Boito, Ponchielli and Verdi. Bottom center, the Treves bookshop. Bottom right, the Piazza del Duomo (Cathedral Square), connected to the Teatro alla Scala's own square by the enclosed Galleria itself.

19

Students together at the Conservatory, with very little in their pockets, Mascagni (left) and Puccini shared lodgings in Milan. In the middle picture at left, they flank Alberto Franchetti at the keyboard. There was talk of rivalry for the same opera subject, I Due Zoccoletti (The Two Wooden Shoes); *bottom, a cartoon of the "quarrel," though in fact they stayed friends.*

IX. PUCCINI AND MASCAGNI—TWO BOHEMIANS

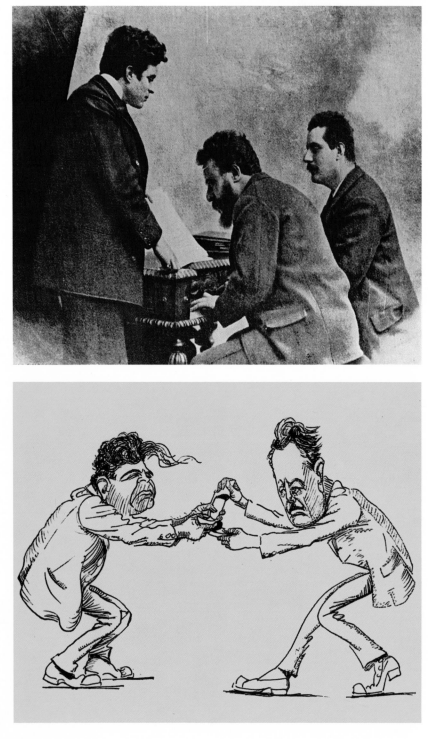

Milan was not Paris. The young artists who were studying and working in the capital of Lombardy were not dreaming of lost paradises, smoking opium and drinking absinthe. To be sure, the young Praga could write strong verses against Manzoni: "Chaste poet, whom Italy worships, old man wrapped up in holy visions, you now can die . . . It is the time of Antichrists, and Christ is dead again." But he didn't carry this facile blasphemy beyond the pale. And for the rest, even one of the major challengers of institutionalized art, Arrigo Boito, had written verses for Verdi's two last masterpieces, *Otello* and *Falstaff.*

No, Milan was not Paris, and the bohemianism that Puccini was living had more the tones of a considered student pose than the desperation of revolt and refusal. Money, as we have seen, was tight. To hold out until the Conservatory diploma arrived, along with the first works of one's pen, it was best to consolidate forces. So Puccini made friends with another student, by this time near the end of his studies—Mascagni, who would become famous for his one-act melodrama *Cavalleria Rusticana* (Rustic Chivalry), based on a story of Sicilian life by Giovanni Verga. Both were Tuscans (Mascagni being from Livorno), both musically gifted, yet Puccini and Mascagni were in fact quite different. The former was contrary, diligent, cautious, not given to dissipation. The latter was a blusterer, always ready for laughter and pranks. For a time the two shared a little apartment on which they had taken a lease together. As soon as they had to go in debt to make the down payment, they figured out a scheme for tricking creditors who came to their door with bills. When one of these showed up looking for Puccini, he would find Mascagni ready to affirm that his friend had just gone out, while actually he was hiding in the clothes closet. The same procedure applied when creditors came looking for Mascagni.

Together they hung out at the cafés downtown, but Puccini was very careful never to overstep his limits. He wrote to his mother, "When I have pocket money, I go to the café, but there are lots of evenings when I don't go, because a drink costs forty *centesimi.*" They took their meals at the Aida Restaurant, where their credit was good: the owner was an opera enthusiast.

Left, a scene from Cavalleria Rusticana, *the one-act opera that brought glory to Mascagni. Directly below, the title page of his score, which he is caricatured conducting at bottom. Lower left, the composer (seated) with members of the cast who gave* Cavalleria *its premiere at the Teatro Costanzi in Rome after it won first prize in a contest.*

A moment of golden opportunity: Theater Illustrated *ran an announcement (at right) for a competition for a one-act opera. Puccini's dream was to win, thereby gaining the stage of* La Scala (below), *a destination granted few young composers. With never a moment to lose, Puccini hoped the opera he would write would please the members* of the distinguished panel of judges for the competition. Among them he already had a few friends, chiefly Ponchielli. The chosen librettist was Ferdinando Fontana, the subject Le Villi (The Wilis). *Puccini wrote fast and produced a more than pleasing work, but he did not win. His consolation prize was a production sponsored by friends.*

INCORAGGIAMENTO
AI GIOVANI COMPOSITORI ITALIANI

CONCORSO.

Il *Teatro Illustrato* apre ai giovani musicisti di nazionalità italiana un concorso per un'opera in un atto di soggetto *idilliaco, serio* o *giocoso,* a scelta del concorrente, col premio di L. 2000, oltre la rappresentazione dell'opera in un teatro di Milano per cura e a spese del giornale.

X. A CONTEST AND THE FIRST OPERA

At length Puccini got his diploma (below), earning a bronze medal and presenting as his senior thesis a Capriccio Sinfonico *(page shown at bottom left), which was conducted by Franco Faccio (caricatured at bottom right), a celebrated conductor who had led the premiere of Verdi's* Otello *and was considered the top man in his profession in Italy. Puccini's piece proved lively and pleasing and drew the critics' attention to the young composer (the daily* Perseveranza *was first to speak of it). Likewise the attention of publishers, who controlled the climate of Italy's musical life, for better or for worse. Puccini later borrowed some of the music of his* Capriccio *for* La Bohème, *to characterize the Bohemians.*

On July 16, 1883, Giacomo Puccini got his diploma in composition from the Milan Conservatory, with a bronze medal. He was exactly twenty-five-and-a-half years old. His thesis composition, *Capriccio Sinfonico* (Symphonic Caprice), was played by the student orchestra under the celebrated Maestro Franco Faccio. It enjoyed a genuine success. Filippo Filippi, one of the most severe and respected critics, who wrote for *La Perseveranza,* openly praised it, emphasizing the "definite and rare musical temperament, especially symphonic" and finding in the composer "unity of style, personality, character." *La Gazzetta Musicale,* published by the House of Ricordi, also praised it and recommended it to the attention of connoisseurs. It soon began to be said that young Puccini would make his mark.

Now was the moment to look for a stroke of luck. This presented itself in the form of a contest organized by the magazine *Il Teatro Illustrato,* published by the Sonzogno firm. It offered a rehearsal, reserved for artists making their debut, for an unpublished one-act opera. On the judges' committee were Amilcare Ponchielli, plus Pietro Platania, Franco Faccio, Cesare Dominicetti and Amintore Galli. So it was comprised of teachers and composers whom Puccini already knew, having met them at the home of his teacher and protector, Ponchielli.

He had to find a good subject and a librettist inclined to take a chance along with the composer. Ponchielli acted as go-between, introducing Puccini to Fernando Fontana, a versifier who had a libretto already in hand. Puccini liked it, finding it "of a symphonic-descriptive kind, which suits me, because it seems sure to work."

The opera was written and presented to the committee. But when the awards were announced, *Le Villi* received not so much as an honorable mention. At this point, Puccini's friends intervened on the side of fate. After the young man had played over his opera at a party at the home of Marco Sala, a wealthy music-lover, Giulio Ricordi and Arrigo Boito, along with other guests, decided it should be staged independently at the Teatro Dal Verme, a smaller theater in Milan. A subscription was set up to cover the expenses of the production. Puccini's dream was shared by his supporters, and it had to come true.

On this page, a photo of Giacomo Puccini around the time of Le Villi, a poster of the Teatro Dal Verme and a view of the inside of that same theater. The Dal Verme could be called a sort of antechamber of La Scala, the temple of opera, after which it was Milan's second most famous theater; Enrico Caruso made his debut there, before moving on to La Scala. Le Villi enjoyed good success with both critics and public. Due notice was taken of the young Maestro's melodic skill and able orchestration. His was a fresh, sincere new talent, even if the opera was a bit naive in the theatrical sense—a sense that would later prove to be one of Puccini's principal assets.

The subscription, first signed by Arrigo Boito, was successful, and the opera by Puccini, his first, was able to be performed. *Le Villi*—a tale about a young man pursued to his death by the Wilis, spirits of girls who had been abandoned by their lovers—went onstage at the Teatro Dal Verme on May 31, 1884. The outcome, with both press and public, was enthusiastic. In fact the score possesses moments of melodic felicity and knowledgeable writing—not much more. The principals lack characterization, and young Puccini was not yet a master of the stage. The publisher Giulio Ricordi, however, who had a nose for talent and trusted his instincts of long standing, decided it suited him to single out this young maestro from Lucca, who showed a sincere disposition toward melody and an unusual capacity for making music. Four days after the premiere, therefore, he called him into his office and proposed to buy the rights to his opera, on the condition it be lengthened to two acts. Not only that, he entrusted him with writing a new opera, and offered him an allowance of 300 lire per month for a year.

This is how the name of Puccini started to make a place for itself in the music world. As for Giuseppe Verdi, the grand old man mentioned the young Tuscan composer in a letter to Count Opprandino Arrivabene: "I've heard a lot of good things about this musician Puccini. I've seen a letter that says all good things about him. He follows the modern trend, and that's natural, but he remains attached to melody, which is neither old-fashioned nor modern." It was an important endorsement, because Verdi was sparing with his praise.

In the meantime, in July of that year, Albina Magi, Giacomo's mother, died. Puccini received word of it in Milan and was devastated. On her grave he placed the laurel wreath he had received the night of the triumph of *Le Villi*. Then, as if to forget, he threw himself into his work. He had the road of his first opera to follow. *Le Villi* was given at La Scala, reworked into two acts, on January 24, 1885, while a month earlier it had been given at the Teatro Regio in Turin. The favorable reception of the Dal Verme in Milan was repeated. The press showed itself very favorably disposed, and so did the public. Puccini moved to a new apartment, on the Piazza Baccaria.

Top, a scene from Le Villi *in a recent production at the Puccini Festival at Torre del Lago. Bottom left, frontispiece of the same opera in its first edition. Above, the final scene, in which the Wilis (spirits of betrayed maidens) drive the faithless lover to his death. Though* Le Villi *showed undeniable promise in portraying theatrical situations, it never succeeded in finding a place in the regular repertory. Despite a couple of effective arias, the score showed a disposition toward symphonic depiction, considered Wagnerian at the time. For Puccini's instinctive talent to develop fully, he needed to find striking stage situations that would make use of the scenic picture and vivid characters—a need he himself recognized, as did his publisher, Giulio Ricordi.*

In the print (top below) showing La Scala as the "Ricordi Factory," a reality of the time was recognized —Ricordi's pervasive influence on the Italian theatrical scene. Bottom left, the real factory of the publishing house, which not only signed the best-known composers but issued its own periodical, La Gazzetta Musicale (The Musical Gazette).

Top right, a photo with Puccini's dedication "To my beloved Signor Giulio Ricordi"; below, the original scores of Puccini's operas in Ricordi's archives. The collaboration between the maestro and his publisher was always a happy one and knew few moments of stress. For his part, Puccini always showed toward Ricordi his esteem and filial affection.

Antica sede della casa editrice G. Ricordi & C. nell'edificio del Teatro alla Scala di Milano

XII. GIULIO RICORDI

More than a publisher, Giulio Ricordi (below) was a psychologist and manager whose instincts guided and protected his pupil, launching his career throughout the world. He overruled his own board of directors, who considered his faith in Puccini excessive. An able man, generally esteemed, diplomatic and reasonable, he sensed how to bring out Puccini's abilities and how to find him the best collaborators, choosing the best from the cultural milieu of the time. Sensitive to subtle shadings, he knew how to deal with a difficult, reclusive composer not unlike the grand old man Giuseppe Verdi in that respect. Though discreet in his advice, Ricordi was sure and firm. He realized that a good publisher was also a psychologist.

Thin, meager, not very tall, with white moustache and goatee, very elegant, rather too carefully dressed, Giulio Ricordi was one of the most important men in Milan. Above all he was Verdi's publisher, and he was very able at developing his knowledge and his image. He didn't hesitate to throw himself, if necessary, into the political arena, and for four years he was a member of the Milan city council. He owned a musical magazine, he was connected with *Il Corriere della Sera* and *La Perseveranza,* but for him actions spoke louder than words. He was cautious and unpredictable at the same time. In a certain sense he was also the boss of La Scala. There was no opera season, whether fall or Carnival, that he did not license to perform his publications. He ran his own business shrewdly, with a hand of iron in a velvet glove. And he knew how to choose his collaborators. He listened to Arrigo Boito a great deal, likewise Giuseppe Giacosa, and the famous conductor Franco Faccio was on his staff. He knew how to maintain good relations with singers: Tamagno, Pasta, Maurel and many others were his friends. Discreet, wary, never categorical in his judgments, he knew how to give advice without seeming too give it. He cultivated Verdi with patient love, with affectionate assiduity. But he knew too that the great composer was an old man, in need of an heir. This he watched for: Mascagni had been taken away from him by Sonzogno, Leoncavallo did not altogether convince him, Catalani he had under contract but sensed he was short of artistic breath and infirm of health.

Now there was this fellow Puccini to be followed attentively. The first duty of a publisher, Ricordi confessed to Boito, was that of knowing how to scout for new talents, to discover them and help them realize their potential. If he decided a young artist needed to be developed, he went ahead of him on his path, looked out for him, helped him in every way, up to the point of pushing him with advice on how to run his life. This happened right on schedule with Puccini. Faced with stockholders who complained that his investment in Puccini seemed too extensive and risky, Ricordi shot back tartly that he himself was more than ready to hand in his resignation.

In sum, he put all his eggs in Puccini's basket. He sensed that Puccini was able to speak to everyone.

Directly below, we see Puccini with his wife, Elvira, and their son, Antonio, at their villa in Torre del Lago. At home, the composer of La Bohème *was a man of regular habits, somewhat close-mouthed about his artistic problems, given to two dominant passions— hunting and automobiles. For the rest, he was content to rely on familiar routine.*

In the lower picture, Puccini and Antonio at the seashore in Viareggio toward the end of the first decade of the twentieth century. As a parent, Puccini was somewhat distracted—generous, wanting the best for his child but incapable of devoting very much time to him, because of the constant preoccupations and anxieties of his work.

XIII. ELVIRA

It is not known exactly when Puccini made the acquaintance of Elvira Gemignani. Perhaps at the time of the first trials of *Le Villi,* during one of his infrequent trips to Lucca. Whenever it was, it had the earmarks of a classic case of love at first sight.

Elvira Gemignani, two years younger than the composer, was a very good-looking woman with proud features, soft blond hair, dark, lively eyes and erect posture. She was married to a pharmacist who had been a schoolmate of Puccini's. She had a daughter and son, Fosca and Renato. It started out with the usual subterfuges, letters, secret meetings, the frame that surrounds all so-called forbidden loves. Then it was no longer possible to hide anything, and scandal broke out in the little provincial city.

After the birth of her third child, Tonio (of whom Puccini was the father) in 1886, the year 1887 had hardly begun when Elvira decided to join Puccini in Milan, taking her daughter along. In Lucca the affair provoked a furious reaction. The city rose up in arms against the lovers, to the point where various relatives of the composer took sides.

To live in Milan, the composer had gone into debt with certain of his relatives. Now he felt renounced and condemned for his liaison with a married woman. Besides, *Le Villi* still produced little in the way of author's rights, and *Edgar,* the new opera his publisher had commissioned, was slow in coming. Puccini worked on it with difficulty, having little feeling for its medieval story and romantic fustian. Ferdinando Fontana's text had some turgid spots, which the love interest did not suffice to alleviate. Moreover, though Elvira showed herself a passionate woman, ready to make any sacrifice for her Giacomo, she was also very restless and possessive. Living together was not easy, and quarrels often broke out. The woman reproved the composer with having given up everything for him, to no purpose. Puccini was discouraged, depressed. He went so far as to think of letting opera go hang, of giving up the struggle. The state of his soul is revealed by these lines he wrote to his brother, Michele, in Argentina: "I don't know how to get ahead. The 300 lire a month from Ricordi isn't enough, and every month I'm turning out bad work up to here—may God set me free!"

Elvira Gemignani (left), mistress and later wife of the composer, was not an ideal mate for the Maestro. She was jealous and irritable, of unstable moods. Furthermore, she had a complex about growing old, feeling herself to be ugly and overweight, while her husband, as he advanced in age, added a touch of elegance and fascination to his own appearance.

Puccini was very much concerned with finding a place where his wife could feel relaxed, so he bought the villa at Chiatri (below), isolated and far from the usual round of daily cares, where he hoped she would settle down into a freer existence. But the idea was not a success beyond the first few months. Her temperament was not suited to relaxation.

For the premiere of Edgar, *the first opera that Puccini wrote for La Scala, Ricordi spared no pains of preparation. The soprano was Amelia Cattaneo (right), who enjoyed a good reputation, and the conductor was Franco Faccio (middle right), the best to be had in Italy, who had guided the fortunes of the first performance of* Le Villi.

Below Left, *cover of the published score of* Edgar, *a work that showed musical refinement and complexity. Drawn from the writings of Alfred de Musset (bottom right),* Edgar *did not fit Musset's stylized romanticism any better than it fit the world that Puccini's next works would soon create, one of credible characters.*

XIV. "EDGAR," A SUCCÈS D'ESTIME

Edgar *(top below, a sketch for the second act by G. Palanti), together with* Le Villi *(bottom, a scene from the Torre del Lago production of 1984) would never enter the regular world repertory; stage performances and recordings have been rare, inspired mainly by curiosity about Puccini's early work. The composer, a romantic who drew his inspiration from credible human feelings, the* inward states of the soul, did not find congenial subjects in either Le Villi *or* Edgar: *their formal, externalized passions did not ring true to him. Yet the resulting operas, though they showed eclectic and conventional traits, also showed an instinctive grasp of dramatic situation, a trait that would emerge to the full in the works of his imminent maturity.*

Fontana, the librettist of *Edgar,* was the same poet who had written the verses of *Le Villi.* The complete libretto was turned over to the composer in May 1885, but the opera was not performed until April 21, 1889. it took Puccini four years to compose the four acts (later revised to three). This was the first and last time that Puccini, with a complete text in his hands, took so much time to write an opera.

In this case, however, he didn't know how to go about it. The opera, adapted from a novel by Alfred de Musset, was from a dramatic standpoint almost nonexistent. It didn't ring true, with its borrowed romantic finery, and the story took place in the fourteenth century, to which the composer was unable to relate. It is a story of pure love ruined by sensuality and by the malevolence of a woman, Tigrana, who does her all to break the bonds that unite Edgar with his gentle Fidelia. There are recognitions, capsized situations, deaths for love, murders for vengeance—everything except a real plot and real characters. Of course, this was a time in Italy when, in the wake of *Lohengrin* and *Tannhäuser,* everyone wanted to revive Nordic and medieval sagas.

The opera's success, if such it was, was solely one of esteem. Some curtain calls between the acts, some applause growing toward the end. The writing was more expert than in *Le Villi,* the melodic line firmer and more originally bodied out. But all the praises stopped there. *Edgar* was too long, with traits bordering on the annoying. Giulio Ricordi quickly took stock of it: it could not have a great future. But he did not take this as a calamity, and he did not give up faith in the composer. On the contrary—he commissioned another opera from him. Having understood the temperament and character of his protégé, he did take away Fontana. For Puccini there were other men of the theater, better able to sketch situations and develop personalities; above all, there were love stories that would ring true. He exhorted him to carry on. Puccini should leave *Edgar* to make its way, which in a sense it did, never altogether disappearing from the repertory. He should never give another thought to this half-baked success but should practice even more, listen to more music and get ready for more work, for the test of his calling, which had to be, and which had to carry the day.

XV. "MANON LESCAUT"

Between *Edgar* and *Manon Lescaut,* three years and ten months ran by. Certainly they were not among Puccini's happiest. On the one hand, there was his wish to recover from the tepid success of *Edgar;* on the other, a sneaking suspicion was growing stronger in his mind that perhaps he was not meant for opera. He thought of emigrating, or of changing occupations, making money from music as an artisan rather than an artist. But Giulio Ricordi didn't give up. First he sent him to Bayreuth, together with the conductor Franco Faccio, to listen to the Wagner operas and decide whether to acquire the rights for the publishing house. Then he commissioned a third opera. And he let him be the artist and decide.

During that period, Puccini was thinking about many plays, reading many possible subjects. For a little while he didn't know what to choose. Ricordi put no pressure on him. Sometimes he would suggest a subject and collaboration with Giacosa, but when the composer declined, the publisher didn't insist.

The choice was Puccini's, and he would choose to compose *Manon Lescaut,* from the Abbé Prevost's novel, already successfully set to music by Jules Massenet. At this point Giulio Ricordi objected that the idea sounded crazy. The opera by the French master had been widely performed and accepted. To put oneself in competition would seem a serious miscalculation. But Puccini already saw clearly what he wanted to do. The first draft of the text was entrusted to Leoncavallo, but then the collaboration between the two broke off. Marco Praga stepped in, turning for versification to the poet Domenico Oliva. But after a period of work, Puccini's requirements weighed too heavily on the pair, who gave up the project. Ricordi then asked for help from Giuseppe Giacosa, who in turn suggested bringing in Luigi Illica. At length the libretto would be published without the authors' names, and it would be three years before Puccini declared himself satisfied.

When it finally came to performance, in Turin on February 1, 1893, the outcome was a triumph. The public inundated the various numbers with applause. Puccini's hand had become surer, his melodic inspiration freer and more refined, his writing agile, spirited, colorful. Now Ricordi knew for sure he had found a successor to Verdi.

After the moderate success of his first two operas, Puccini knew real triumph with Manon Lescaut. Asserting himself as an artist, he had chosen the subject himself and supervised its preparation. Recognizing the high stakes, Giulio Ricordi spared nothing for the production—not the interpreters (bottom left, Cesira Ferrani in the title role) or the posters (left and top right), not the press promotion or the timing of the premiere at the Teatro Regio in Turin (bottom right), coincidential with the premiere of Verdi's Falstaff at La Scala in Milan. The carefully orchestrated campaign paid off, and Puccini, who up till then had been a promising name, was a celebrity. Many considered him Verdi's rightful heir.

The chalet of Torre del Lago, as it looked in Puccini's day (right) and as it looks today (below). Retiring and solitary by nature, the composer loved to take refuge here, feeling at home amid the cycles of nature—water, sky, open countryside and an abundance of quiet. This was his true domain, his kingdom, and he could not ask for more.

34

XVI. THE HOUSE AT TORRE DEL LAGO

Once he had achieved financial security, the composer bought a house at Torre del Lago (middle picture, as it was; bottom, as it is now). At right, his studio is preserved as he used it. Little by little, this villa became his home base. Here he wrote the better part of his music, on this piano, with a view over the lake.

The success of *Manon Lescaut* produced two results for the composer—one material, the other moral. The material one was that financial luck had finally struck. So much for debts, anxiety, prayers to have enough. Now Puccini was rich; his royalties yielded well, *Manon Lescaut* was requested by major theaters all over the world, and Ricordi placed himself more and more at his service. In May 1895, George Bernard Shaw, music critic for *The World,* wrote after hearing *Manon Lescaut,* "Italian opera has been born again," adding that "Puccini looks to me more like the heir of Verdi than any of his rivals." Puccini felt this too, and it made him surer of himself from the point of view of morale. It cancelled out his beginner's doubts and anxieties, made him more sanguine and exigent toward the development of his work. The first result of Puccini's economic good fortune was that he could buy a house—a villa, rather—at Torre del Lago, not right in Lucca but near enough. And there he took refuge. At heart he was a hermit, a man who disliked city life and was disenchanted with Milan, which was becoming more and more a thriving metropolis, full of traffic, work, discord and trouble. Puccini liked nature, hunting, the silence of a landscape surrounded by mountains and opening up toward the sea. He took refuge at Torre del Lago, then, with Elvira, with whom his rapport was always wavering between idyll and drama. Elvira was obsessed with jealousy. Her Giacomo had become a handsome man, and fame added to his charm. But, at least for the moment, there were no dangerous rivals at Torre del Lago. So he, the young maestro barely kissed by Lady Luck, could relax his nerves, unburden himself, go hunting, live the way he liked and lay plans for his next work. Because now that he had entered the halls of glory, he had to stay there. And if one success is hard to match, maintaining it runs the risk of becoming even more successful. He continued to read a lot, especially plays and novels by contemporary writers, and in his mind he worked on a thousand projects. At a certain point he let himself be tempted by a typical verist drama, *La Lupa* (The She-Wolf) by Giovanni Verga. But then he gave it up. He already had his eye on a book by the French journalist Henry Mürger, *Scènes de la Vie de Bohème* (Scenes of Bohemian Life).

Two scenes designed by A. Ferri for Loreley *in a production at La Scala, and (right) a portrait of the composer, Alfredo Catalani. Like Puccini, he was a native of Lucca, and for a time he was considered the new man in Italian music; but his success never grew beyond a certain point. Refined, poetic and sensitive, his music lacked the dramatic aptitude and* popular appeal of Puccini's. Not without reason, Catalani resented the desertion of his publisher, Giulio Ricordi, in favor of promoting Puccini's operas. Slightly older than Puccini, Catalani did not begrudge his compatriot's success but felt deprived of his own fair share. He died relatively young, knowing his star had waned.*

XVII. RIVALRY WITH CATALANI

Alfredo Catalani, composer of *La Wally* and *Loreley,* was a fellow Luccan four years older than Puccini. He came from a background less tinged with poverty. Musically gifted, intelligent, sensitive, enamored of Wagnerian experiments and the Nordic school of music, linked with bohemianism, after his studies at the Milan Conservatory he had gotten off to a promising start. At first, with urging from Arrigo Boito, the publisher Ricordi singled him out as the successor to Verdi. Then, with Ricordi's intuition for the lyric stage, for what the public liked and wanted, he shifted his support to Puccini. Catalani was relegated to neglect by his publishing house, which didn't push his work, or pushed it very little, saving its concern for his younger rival. Only Arturo Toscanini, bound to Catalani by great friendship, stayed loyal to him. To make a living, there was nothing for the composer to do except teach.

Sick with tuberculosis, lacking the soul of a fighter, too sensitive and introverted, Catalani—who had written some beautiful music and even an opera that would last (that is, *La Wally*)—didn't know how to claim the recognition he deserved. His music, so in-

Catalani's best-known opera, La Wally *(title page below), still occasionally performed in Italy today, is a score of orchestral delicacy and power, with a strong, expressive role for the leading soprano. At left, Arturo Toscanini, drawn by L. Bemporad while conducting the Verdi Requiem on the occasion of Verdi's centenary. As long as Toscanini was responsible for musical leadership at La Scala, La Wally had its due in the theater's repertory. Though Toscanini was friendly with Puccini, he had been an early champion of Catalani as well, and was with the discouraged Catalani when he died. In his NBC Symphony years he continued to play Catalani's works.*

gratiating and gentle, so full of contrasts and sprinkles of light, so lean, convinced the public less and less, though it deserved their attention. It never filled theaters, and the composer never drew acclaim. He grew steadily sicker, more depressed, more tired of always having to start over again. Toscanini promoted him, specifying his operas whenever invited to conduct. What Toscanini could not specify was enthusiastic success, acclaim, public attention. In February 1893, a few months before Catalani died, he expressed himself this way in a letter to a critic: "All the newspapers are for Puccini, all the theaters as well. Lucky him, to have known how to make his mark; I never succeeded in doing it! At Brescia they were supposed to give *La Wally* this year, and instead . . . I swear to you, I wouldn't mind if I didn't see partiality on Ricordi's part. There should be room in the world for everyone; but that's not what they think there, in that house."

Poor Catalani! More and more forgotten, he died in the month of August 1893, in a Milan abandoned by people on summer holiday, in the arms of his one true friend, Arturo Toscanini.

LA WALLY
DI W. DE HILLERN
RIDUZIONE DRAMMATICA
in 4 atti
DI
L. ILLICA
MUSICA
di
A. CATALANI
EDIZIONI RICORDI
(Printed in Italy)

Right, scene from the third act of La Bohème *that decorates a silver cigarette case owned by Puccini. Middle left, the last act as staged in Paris in 1899; to its right, costume sketches for Mimi and Marcello. Bottom left, Mimi's death scene as designed and staged by Franco Zeffirelli at La Scala. And bottom right, poster promoting* the world premiere production at the Theatro Regio in Turin. One of the best-loved of all operas, La Bohème *has never flagged in popularity throughout the world, ranking with* Aida, *the opera that first fired Puccini's determination to compose. Not only is the score a masterpiece, but the characters represent youth itself.*

XVIII. "LA BOHÈME"

Youth is fleeting: La Bohème *is a drama, but it is also a love song, with characters like ourselves, with our own hopes and dreams and problems. Liked from the first by the public, it used to be held in suspicion by the critics, who in recent years have acknowledged its great qualities. The work can be read on various levels. One can listen for the spontaneity of its outbursts of melody, but one can also savor its delicate shadings and details. Upper picture, the third-act quartet as imagined in a print of the period; bottom, a caricature by the singer Autori of the cast of the 1925 La Scala production, prepared under the regime of Arturo Toscanini just after the composer's death.*

By now, Puccini had figured everything out. He knew what the public wanted, and how to give it to them. He knew that opera is music but also theater— that is, in a sense of action, incisiveness, characters and personalities, good timing.

To achieve this, he chose a subject, *Scenes of Bohemian Life,* from Henry Mürger's novel, and chose the librettists, Luigi Illica and Giuseppe Giacosa. In the three years that ran from the premiere of *Manon Lescaut* to that of *La Bohème,* he gave his collaborators no rest. To do scenes over he took out verses, added, put his foot down. Giacosa reached the limits of his patience, confessing to Ricordi, "With the continual revising, retouching, adding, correcting, cutting, abbreviating, fattening to the right so as to slim to the left, I'm dead tired." But the ordeal went on. Puccini begged and prayed, ordered and coaxed. Among other things, he learned that Leoncavallo was working on an opera on the same subject, with the same title, but this did not faze him. In a letter to *Il Corriere della Sera* he wrote, "Maestro Leoncavallo is setting it to music, and so shall I. Let the public be the judge."

He was sure of himself. He knew that this time would be the determining one. Four times the libretto was completely done over. He had the music in his mind, he ordered the exact sounds and meters, and he said to Giacosa, "Here I'd like verses that have these accents: da-da-da-*da,* da-da-da-*da,* da-*da*-da." And Giacosa turned out the words for Musetta's waltz, "Quando me'n vo, quando me'n vo soletta."

Finally *La Bohème* reached the stage, at the Teatro Regio in Turin, February 1, 1896. Arturo Toscanini conducted. The orchestra seats and boxes were a *Who's Who.* Ricordi had done his work well: the press was there from all over the world, and it was a big, warm public success. The critics, on the other hand, were not so enthusiastic. Carlo Bersezio of *La Stampa* wrote, "*La Bohème* will make no great mark on the history of the lyric stage." It was one of history's many misjudgments. Not only did Puccini's *La Bohème* become known very quickly, from one theater to another, from one country to another, but it was a masterpiece, something quite perfect from both the musical and the theatrical points of view—something, in short, that would endure.

| PERTILE (Rodolfo) | ZAMBONI (Mimì) | FERRARIS (Musetta) | FRANCI (Marcello) | AUTORI (Colline) | PACI (Schaunard) |

Operas are usually the work of two people, a composer and librettist; but for a while Puccini worked successfully as part of a trio. He himself was the real theater man, in the sense of understanding the pulse of the musical stage. His partners were Giuseppe Giacosa, a littérateur with the gift for the poetic turn of phrase, and Liugi Illica, an idea man with a knowledge of drama. Directly below, an autograph by the three for Rosina Storchio, who sang the first Madama Butterfly. Bottom left, Illica's last picture with Puccini; next to it, a fanciful caricature of Giacosa that appeared in the printed edition of his theater work Il Burattinaio (The Puppet Master).

XIX. ILLICA AND GIACOSA

The collaboration on *La Bohème* had been long, hard and tortuous. Puccini had shown himself hard to please, and he would continue to be so. Yet the collaborators complemented each other. Puccini was the one who saw clearly and knew exactly what he wanted. At the same time, he was the most tormented man, the artist curious about everything, who followed every musical trend there was in the world, who had a capacity for writing with refinement and simplicity at the same time. Giacosa for his part had great experience, and elegant mastery of the Italian language and a decadent sensitivity that had often nourished itself from familiarity with French literature. Besides, he had great psychological insight; he understood what motivated the tormented human soul. They called him the Buddha, because he was big, fat and imposing. When he argued with Puccini and resigned in earnest, Giulio Ricordi played him some bars of the opera that was having its birth pangs. At the end, Giacosa exclaimed, "Puccini has surpassed my expectations! Now I understand his tyranny about verses and accents."

As for the third partner, Luigi Illica represented the unpredictable, the touch of irregularity, the love of the pulse-beat, the ability to put together very clear dramatic situations and contrasts. He had ability, we would say today, as a scenographer. He had a sense of action, and if sometimes he ran the risk of being rhetorical, Puccini usually seconded his judgment. Illica was a poet, though little of his work would last, a playwright, a journalist. He was the author of librettos for other composers, but the summit for him was the collaboration with Puccini and Giacosa.

The man who understood all this, who took account of the fact that this was a winning trio, one that couldn't be touched or disturbed, was Giulio Ricordi. His instincts as a publisher told him that sooner or later the collaboration would have to end, that overworking the vein would exhaust it, that it would be necessary to offer Giacomo new challenges, new themes. Partly because that's the way the opera world is made, partly too because Puccini was one who would always want to go forward, to renew himself. But until that happened, blessed be the arguments, blessed be the despair of one or another of the triumvirate.

The three men, different as they were, had in common their psychological insight into stage characters and their feeling for creating something quite new. They first collaborated rather by chance on Manon Lescaut, *the work of many hands, and regularized their partnership for* La Bohème, *cementing it further with* Tosca *and raising it to new heights in* Madama Butterfly. *But results were not achieved without arguments and crises, followed by reconciliations under Giulio Ricordi's guidance. Left, another picture of Giuseppe Giacosa; below left, the saturnine Giacosa flanked by Puccini and Illica; below right, a caricature of the same three, crowned by wreathlike halos suggesting the inspiration that united them.*

This is how Puccini referred to his two collaborators in a letter to Giulio Ricordi: "You will have seen Illica. Now I'm waiting for cuts and revisions from Giacosa. . . . I've made him shorten it— he will have to prune the other's work. It would be a good idea for you too to give it a look, to clear away certain odd twists that really aren't essential, plus quite a few more that Illica clings to like his own children (if he had any) . . . Many cordial greetings, in expectation of a new look at the Latin Quarter, shortened and straightened out with the intervention of the Giacosian Buddha. . ."

Sybil Seligman, in a portrait by the charmingly knowing hand of Giovanni Boldini. She was a discreet friend to Puccini, who found in her comfort, understanding, help and friendship; with her he was able to be always sincere, to confide in her under all circumstances. Their love affair did not last long but soon transformed itself into a reliable, intelligent communication. For Puccini, Sybil went to see plays that were given in London, suggested plots, read books, kept him constantly posted. Between the two there unfolded a correspondence, still not fully or widely known, that offers a great deal of insight into the composer's life, his state of mind and his working methods.

XX. THE ENGLISHWOMAN

A weakness—and what a weakness!—for women he had always had. Puccini didn't know how to resist feminine temptation. If it wasn't a soprano, it was a ballerina. If it wasn't a ballerina, it was a society lady. And imagine what advantage he took of being one of the best-known, most beloved and idolized men in Italy. Yet at heart he was a sad, lonely man, one who got bored when he wasn't working. Women for him represented a pastime—one that sometimes threatened to take him away from music, to the point where his publisher Ricordi once wrote him, "But is it possible that a man like Puccini, such an artist who makes millions tremble . . . could become a useless plaything in the meretricious hands of a vulgar, unworthy woman?"

Aside from his wife, Puccini never had very long relationships with other women. One alone knew how to keep his friendship, even after the love interest had ended—Sybil Seligman, wife of a prominent London banker, who had a nice soprano voice and was an opera enthusiast. Puccini met her at the home of the composer Francesco Paolo Tosti. Between the two a passion developed that went on to transform itself into a solid, longtime friendship. A woman of intelligence, cultured and refined, Sybil became not only his friend, to whom he unburdened himself, but also his counselor and confidante, even in personal, private matters. With her, Puccini succeeded in opening up and being himself. To her he declared his moments of sadness and anxiety, fear and emptiness. From her he asked important advice about the choice of subjects to set to music, books to read. Sybil was always there for him, delicate and discreet, attentive and watchful.

Between the two there sprang up a copious correspondence that lasted about twenty years, until the composer's death. In every letter of Puccini's can be found phrases like "You who are so fond of me," "You who know me better than anyone," "You who know everything about me, and from whom I hide nothing." He confided to her his plans and discouragements, the jealousy with which his wife plagued him, his preferences and idiosyncrasies. To this woman, who stayed in the background, Puccini owed the knowledge that there was someone who cared for him without asking anything in return.

42

Left, a photo of Giacomo Puccini in middle age. Below left, a view of the Thames River in London, as seen from St. Thomas' Hospital; upper right, the Valentino in Turin. These were places where Puccini and Sybil Seligman met to talk, to be together. Puccini would not have known what to do without the friendship of this special person, who always seemed to know the right thing to say to him, the right solution to his problems, and who was always ready to give him her attention. Bottom right, Ingrid Thulin and Alberto Lionello as Sybil and Puccini in a television screenplay. Such was Sybil's tact that she also maintained friendly relations with Puccini's wife.

The upper picture shows Puccini stationed in a rowboat among the reeds of Lake Massaciuccoli, ready to hunt ducks. Below, with friends and his wife, Elvira, in an automobile, preparing for an outing, with the chauffeur at left. Right, a special hunting permit issued as a favor to the Maestro. Hunting and driving, plus motorboating, were the favorite pastimes of Puccini when he was not working. He would rise early in the morning and walk long distances to intercept the pathways flown by wild game birds. As a shot he was more enthusiastic than accurate. Hunting and driving—though the latter cost him a serious accident— offered an excuse to escape domestic tensions.

XXI. TWO PASSIONS: HUNTING AND AUTOMOBILES

On the shore of Lake Massaciuccoli stood a hunting lodge called the Bohème Club, where Puccini could meet with cronies from various walks of life and indulge in impromptu parties. Puccini felt at ease in such surroundings, which he preferred to the insupportable round of meetings and social affairs forced upon him by city life. Lower picture: the hunting corner of the villa (now a museum) at Torre del Lago. Hanging beside the gun cabinet is the famous picture of Puccini with his librettists Giacosa and Illica. Fascinated by mechanical devices of all sorts, Puccini appreciated fine rifles and ordered various models from factories both in Italy and abroad.

Writing from Paris toward the end of 1899, Giacomo Puccini expressed himself in these terms: "I'm fed up with Paris! I hate pavements! I hate palaces! I have the capitals of columns! I hate fashion! I hate steam, stovepipe hats, tailcoats!" The fact was that, more than the inventions of the modern world, Puccini hated the city, where he felt like a prisoner, where it wasn't easy for him to be alone, where he felt out of touch with nature. For him, instead of the chaos of urban traffic, what was addictive was the panorama of the open countryside, hills that start to look blue and turn into mountains in the distance, the seacoast —especially in winter, when the sky is endlessly gray, and the spray of the waves is sand-colored. There he could dress as he liked, in what agreed with him: ample, comfortable velvet jackets, thick wool trousers, boots, a soft hat just before sunset, a soft scarf around his throat.

And he could go hunting. Hunting was a passion of his; he owned some of the finest double-barreled shotguns yet made, he had very alert dogs, he knew all the trails and footpaths, he knew when the ducks and skylarks passed over, and he knew where to find snipe. But more than shooting (he would never be a first-class shot) he loved to walk and be alone. It was for this he felt the urge to go hunting. For this he needed only a few things—a dog, a rifle, the open countryside and eventually some game. Nothing else. He appeared to be a man of simple habits and tastes, congenial, open, ready for laughter and pranks. Underneath he proved to be a shy man, possessed of an exacerbated sensitivity, of an almost unhealthy vulnerability. That is why he liked to be alone at Torre del Lago, just a country place and nothing more. There his vulnerability felt protected, from both a physical and a psychological viewpoint, and he found shelter from the hated commerce that inevitably went with big cities, and with what it represented to his eyes—daily encounters, pleasantries, crowds, gala dinners, appointments, etiquette. Thus too is explained another passion of his—driving the first motorcars. Puccini bought numerous cars and motorboats, because they provided another means of getting away by himself, of escaping the constraints of living in society, while asserting some personal power and autonomy.

Two scenes from Tosca *in two different La Scala productions: with Placido Domingo in Act III (upper picture) under the baton of Seiji Ozawa, and an earlier performance with Tito Gobbi as Scarpia and Renata Tebaldi as Tosca, Act II, conducted by Victor De Sabata. Filled with melodies that have become very popular on their own,* Tosca *is one of Puccini's three most popular opera, along with* La Bohème *and* Madama Butterfly. *It is not his most typical work, however, for the sentimental elements take second place to the brutal events of Victorien Sardou's contrived, melodramatic plot. Perhaps for this reason, the moments of gentler emotion are especially highly prized.*

XXII. "TOSCA"

The composition of *Tosca* took most of four years—that is, three years and nine months. Puccini had seen the play by Victorien Sardou, and his sense of theater led him to consider this rather truculent, shrill text. For the styling of the libretto he trusted the usual pair, Illica and Giacosa. The usual scenes resumed among the collaborators. Puccini implored, urged, changed his moods, his ideas. He wanted everything better organized, the scenes more tightly structured, the characters more in focus.

As usual, Giacosa was the first to lose patience. He got angry, threatened to quit, did quit. He pulled out of the project. The two librettists complained, among other things, about having to work in the dark—without being able, that is, to hear any of the music Puccini composed to their verses. But on this point Ricordi was precise and strict: he wanted no hints to leak out in advance, and no one (except obviously the composer and himself) should know the melodies of the new Puccini opera. Then there was a difference of opinion between publisher and composer about the third act, which Ricordi found scrappy and weak, while Puccini stoutly defended it. In sum, the usual things already well known whenever Puccini was absorbed in work, with a certain added hypochondria, a sense of depression. To his wife, who was staying in the city, he wrote, "The weather is cloudy, no hunting, I bend my back over the table, writing and scoring, burrowing like a mole for my *Tosca*."

Tosca went onstage at the Teatro Costanzi in Rome on January 14, 1900. The new century was only two weeks old. The theater was filled with the fanciest people to be found in Italy—first among them Queen Margherita, then cabinet ministers, musicians, nobles, newspapermen, publishers. As usual, success sprang loose suddenly, starting with the tenor's first aria, "Recondita armonia." And when Tosca's "Vissi d'arte" arrived in the second art, success was assured. At the end there were seven curtain calls onstage, three of them just for the composer. It was a case of another hit, with some differences from his previous operas: there was the accustomed marvelous melodic line of Puccini, but some cruelty and sadism also reared their heads. Apart from that, Puccini for the first time brought to life a major baritone figure, that of Baron Scarpia, the chief of secret police.

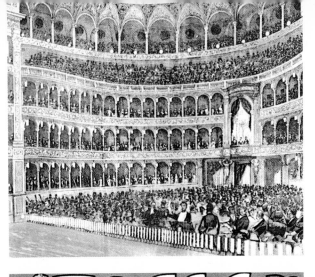

Left, the auditorium of the Teatro Costanzi in Rome, where the first performance of Tosca took place under tense circumstances worthy of the plot. The audience was laced with important figures from the worlds of art and politics; dissidents took advantage of the situation and threatened disruption, but the evening ended in triumph. Middle left, an Art Nouveau poster announcing the work. Bottom left, a caricature by Lionello Cappiello showing Puccini (left) at rehearsal next to Victorien Sardou, playwright of the original drama, with Giulio Ricordi and conductor Leopoldo Mugnone. Below, the impressive Te Deum that closes Act I, as seen at La Scala in the 1978-79 season.

After Manon Lescaut, La Bohème and Tosca, *a fourth success was expected with* Madama Butterfly. *Instead the audience at La Scala erupted in catcalls, whistles, animal noises, wisecracks and laughter. This was Puccini's only outright fiasco, caused by the novelty of the work, which needed (and got) some adjustments to realize its effect. Right,* design by Labò for the stage set. *Middle right, costume designs for La Scala. Lower left, the composer with Elsa Szamosi, Hungarian interpreter of the title role, in 1906. Bottom middle, Giovanni Zenatello and Giuseppe De Luca, co-stars of the disastrous premiere; to the right, Rosetta Pampanini, a famous Butterfly before World War II.*

XXIII. "BUTTERFLY"— FIASCO AND REBIRTH

Scarcely three months later, Madama Butterfly tried her wings for a second flight, this time successful, at Brescia. Apart from some cuts to speed the action, Puccini had redivided the work from two acts into three, which suited the public better. Though he had faith in the opera's worth, Puccini was badly shaken by the fiasco, so

Butterfly's redemption was especially helpful to his self-esteem. After the thunderous drama of Tosca he had dared to try something different, a gradually built-up tragedy on a small, personal, domestic scale, its dominant scene that of Butterfly's long wait for her husband's return. The work's delicacy is its strength.

After the success of *Tosca,* Puccini had to think about a new work. In London in 1900 he attended, without knowing a word of English, a performance of David Belasco's play *Madame Butterfly,* and though he could grasp only the essentials of the plot, he was fascinated by it. A year later, plus or minus a month, he charged Luigi Illica with reading Belasco's script and the story by John Luther Long that had inspired it. Now the machinery was set in motion. After a month, Belasco signed over the rights to Puccini, and Illica and Giacosa were able to start their usual work. Strange to say, he left them to work in blessed peace. Meanwhile, he fought with his wife, who was making life unlivable with her continual jealous scenes. True, there was the usual letter of resignation from Giacosa, but things worked out, and *Butterfly* moved ahead, even if the publisher Ricordi didn't show enthusiasm for the enterprise.

The night of February 17, 1904, marked the premiere at La Scala. The role of the protagonist was entrusted to a star, Rosina Storchio. Everyone expected a triumph, but instead it was a colossal flop. The elegant hall, designed by Giuseppe Piermarini, turned into an inferno for Puccini: the public made fun, shouted, clamored, burst out laughing. The day after, the opera was withdrawn by the publisher. Puccini wrote in a letter, "I feel calm enough in the face of the shame of this commotion, because I feel I've written a live and sincere work, which will surely rise again. I have that conviction."

Three months later, trimmed of certain excesses, revised, redivided in three acts instead of two, *Madama Butterfly* was staged again, at the Teatro Grande in Brescia on the evening of May 28. And it came into its own. *Butterfly* was accepted by the public, which gave it an enthusiastic reception. A good five selections had to be encored, and the composer was called before the footlights a dozen times. Even if it lacked the enchanted perfection of *La Bohème,* its intact purity, *Madama Butterfly* is still a masterwork, especially when the heroine is onstage. Puccini's skill at coloration and timbre furthermore had been sharpened, and his sensitivity, so gentle and tormented, succeeded in communicating directly with the public, telling them of the drama of the love and death of the little geisha.

MADAMA BUTTERFLY
(DA JOHN L. LONG E DAVID BELASCO) — TRAGEDIA GIAPPONESE
~ DI L. ILLICA E G. GIACOSA · MUSICA DI
GIACOMO PUCCINI
G. RICORDI £ C - EDITORI

Though he went back to his hometown as a conquering hero of the musical world, Puccini found he was not readily forgiven for the scandal he had caused in his youth, carrying on an affair with the wife of a former schoolmate, a local pharmacist, and eloping with her to Milan. After the death of her husband, Puccini was able to marry his Elvira, but the mantle of respectability was not cut to either his measure or hers by the conservative citizens of Lucca. Marital relations did not proceed on a serene plateau for Puccini, whose wife was extremely jealous, and he often sought the healing solitude of the wilderness in the surrounding countryside, at Torre del Lago or Chiatri; but life in the country did little to calm Elvira.

XXIV. THE DRAMA OF DORIA MANFREDI

Doria Manfredi had been hired as a nurse in the Puccini household (to help the Maestro when he was recuperating from an auto accident), then kept on as a maid. The new century was three years old, and the darkest period in the life of Giacomo Puccini was about to begin. His relations with Elvira, whom he married in 1904 after the death of her first husband, were always on the verge of breaking down. Elvira treated her dependents badly, continually creating scenes in front of everyone, and raised her voice against her husband for his repeated infidelities. Then she took aim at young Doria, a gentle girl who idolized Puccini, and who was always a willing worker. It doesn't appear there was ever any relationship between the Maestro and the housemaid. The fact remains that Elvira suddenly imagined her suspicions to be true and started to torment poor Doria, accusing her of "immoral conduct" and claiming to have caught her *in flagrante* with Puccini.

The girl was fired. But not content with that, Elvira went around Torre del Lago labeling her a good-for-nothing and even demanding that the local priest send her out of his parish. Puccini took refuge in Paris, trying to immerse himself in work, but his absence did not relieve the situation, and it came to a head. The poor girl, persecuted and slandered by Elvira, took poison in her mother's house on January 23, 1909, and killed herself. Scandal broke out, and Doria Manfredi's family sued Puccini's wife. After several months, the trial took place, and Elvira was held guilty of defamation, injuries and threats, with a sentence of five days in prison, 700 lire in damages and the costs of the trial. As a matter of course an appeal was filed, but before a new trial could be set up, Puccini offered 12,000 lire to the poor girl's family if they would withdraw the charges. In that way the matter was shelved.

The man and the artist emerged sorely tried by this ordeal. Puccini had a nervous breakdown, gave up writing for a while, and his relations with his wife continued to hover on the brink of collapse. But never was Puccini tempted by the idea of divorce. "I've passed the most tragic days of my life," he wrote to Sybil. "Now I feel better, but it turns my stomach to think of the wrongs that have been done." And then: "My existence is torture!"

It was in the very spot that Puccini had chosen as a refuge that the housemaid Doria Manfredi, unjustly accused of "immoral conduct" by Elvira, took her own life, precipitating a national scandal and protracted lawsuit. Left, a photo of the poor girl printed with her funeral notice. Below left, the singer Nada playing Doria Manfredi in Sandro Bolchi's drama about Puccini for Italian television; to her right, Elvira Puccini, instigator of the tragedy. Bottom left, view of Lake Massaciuccoli at Torre del Lago, where Puccini—who had spent some of his happiest days there—now spent some of his most miserable. Bottom right, a room in the Puccini villa (today a museum), where the unfortunate Doria worked as nurse and domestic.

Right, the Metropolitan Opera House in New York as it looked at the time of Puccini's visit. Below, the Maestro walking on the Brooklyn Bridge, then nearly completed. Bottom left, David Belasco, from whose play The Girl of the Golden West *the next Puccini opera would evolve. Center, an American cartoon showing the composer delivering his newest creation to New York. Right,* a typical New York street scene of the era. Though he understood little English, Puccini felt at home in this bustling city; its enterprise might have reminded him of the more irritating aspects of Milan or Paris, but society millionaires and the local Italian community, especially singers and other musicians of his acquaintance, feted him with cordiality.

THIS IS COMPOSER PUCCINI.

XXV. TRIP TO AMERICA

To publicize his work, Puccini was willing to let his picture be used for dignified advertising. In one instance he wrote a testimonial (in French) saying he had used the Waterman fountain pen exclusively in composing La Fanciulla del West and found it a superb instrument. For his endorsement of the Knabe, official piano of the Metropolitan Opera for many decades, he allowed the copywriter to go beyond this message into a realm of almost D'Annunzian poetic hyperbole. The Knabe ad (below) duly appeared on the back cover of printed librettos sold at the opera house. Though it may smack of unseemly exploitation to some, this form of endorsement was common practice among performing artists, including singers at the Met.

For six years Puccini didn't write a note. This had never happened to him before. The ongoing crisis over Doria Manfredi, the payments he derived from his success and fame, wealth and continual struggles with his wife, the habitual collaboration with Illica and Giacosa that now seemed to have reached its end, and the old age of Giulio Ricordi, who was getting ready to hand over the reins to his son, Tito—all this, together with the passing of years and the sadness they brought, rendered Puccini silent. During this period he made many plans and looked at many proposed subjects—*Romeo and Juliet,* the life of St. Margaret of Cortona, Oscar Wilde's *A Florentine Tragedy,* Daudet's stories about Tartarin de Tarascon, a Marie Antoinette story.

Giuseppe Giacosa died, and not only was this a source of grief for Puccini, it also brought on the feeling of growing old, which followed threateningly at his heels. He needed to renew, to reactivate himself. Perhaps he would have less impetus than before, but he was still a major artist, a tormented human being. He traveled around, heard music by new composers, such as Debussy's *Pelléas et Mélisande,* which left him disconcerted, impressed by this new way of writing. Things were changing in the artistic world; a revolution was coming that would have far-reaching effects. Even if they were not clear to him, Puccini sensed these things, and they combined to put him into a crisis.

It was during this period that he was invited to New York to supervise the first Metropolitan Opera productions of *Manon Lescaut* and *Madama Butterfly.* This was in reality a publicity gimmick. The stay in New York delighted Puccini. American vitality, the myth of the Western frontier that was still going on (this was in 1907), the city crowds, the skyscrapers, all seemed to push him toward a new strength, a wish to express himself anew, to write again. He met with David Belasco, who had given him the point of departure for *Madama Butterfly,* and became interested in *The Girl of the Golden West,* a play similar to a serialized newspaper novel. For Puccini it was fascinating, this strong-hued tale that unfolded in a land so far and different from his own, this plot that opens in a saloon during the Gold Rush. This is how he decided on his seventh opera.

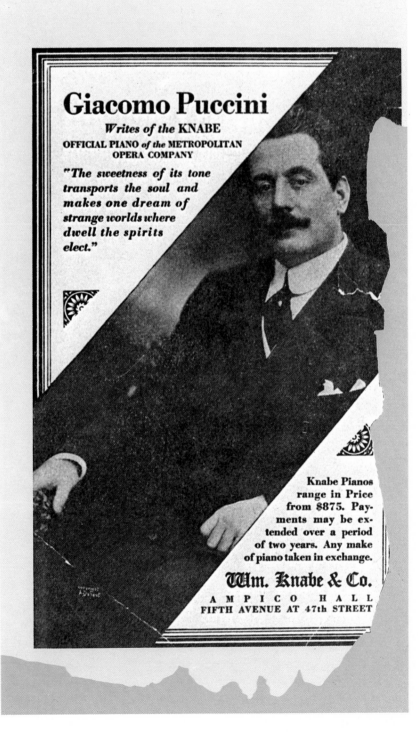

The prime movers of the premiere production of La Fanciulla del West: *Giulio Gatti-Casazza, general manager of the Metropolitan Opera; David Belasco, playwright and stage director, who created the original play and recreated it for the opera stage; Arturo Toscanini, principal conductor of the Italian wing at the opera house; and Giacomo Puccini, whose enthusiasm for an American subject overcame all misgivings on the part of his publisher and colleagues. Like Dvorák with his* New World Symphony, *Puccini listened to the songs of America and recaptured their nostalgia in his own terms. His work was a modern opera such as no American composer had been able to write: with his instinct for the stage, Puccini showed the way.*

XXVI. "LA FANCIULLA DEL WEST"

Returning to Italy, Puccini spoke with Giulio Ricordi and got his agreement, thought it was less than enthusiastic. But the Maestro didn't start harboring doubts. He had decided to go forward on his chosen path. He knew that the more time passed, the more difficult the task would become. He also knew he could not allow himself the luxury of reworking the text himself. He had to change collaborators: Giacosa was no more, and relations with Illica had gone downhill, so for a scenario he turned to the not very well-known Carlo Zangarini. And the usual business began—Puccini's working and reworking, his usual state of never being satisfied. He felt that this opera, as he put it, could be "another *Bohème,* but stronger, more passionate, broader in scope." He needed the librettist to give him something to work with, however—to approach it as he himself did—and this did not always happen. Then Puccini would get fed up, would try to distract himself and find inspiration by traveling (in reality he was fleeing from Elvira, whose nagging never let up), even to Egypt. Then he decided to stop working with Zangarini and entrusted the libretto to Guelfo Civinini, a reporter for *Il Corriere della Sera.* One month after another, with hard work (to renew oneself is a heavy assignment, calling for a great expenditure of energy), with feverish outbursts, *La Fanciulla* finally reached completion. Puccini was happy with it. He wrote to Sybil, "*The Girl* is a success—for me, my best work." In fact it was a rich score, in which the orchestra was treated with notable skill, with evident mastery of harmony and sonority. After the figure of Scarpia in *Tosca,* here was the second important baritone role in Puccini's work, that of the sheriff Jack Rance. And the female protagonist too had something quite new among Puccini's heroines: she was stronger, tougher, more deeply characterized.

The premiere took place at the Metropolitan Opera on November 10, 1910. The cast was splendid—Emmy Destinn, Enrico Caruso, Pasquale Amato, with Toscanini on the podium. The outcome was a triumph to the *n*th degree, one of epic proportions: fourteen curtain calls after the first act, nineteen after the second, a great manifestation at the end. Puccini had won again.

GRAND OPERA SEASON 1910-1911
GIULIO GATTI-CASAZZA, General Manager
Saturday Evening, December 10, 1910, at 8 o'clock.
SPECIAL PERFORMANCE—FIRST TIME ON ANY STAGE

THE GIRL OF THE GOLDEN WEST
(LA FANCIULLA DEL WEST)
(In Italian)
OPERA IN THREE ACTS.——Libretto by G. ZANGARINI and C. CIVINNI.
Founded on the Drama written by DAVID BELASCO.
Music by GIACOMO PUCCINI.

MINNIE	EMMY DESTINN
DICK JOHNSON, (Ramerrez, the road-agent)	ENRICO CARUSO
JACK RANCE, Gambler and Sheriff	PASQUALE AMATO
NICK, Bartender at the "Polka"	ALBERT REISS
ASHBY, Wells-Fargo Agent	ADAMO DIDUR
SONORA	DINH GILLY
TRIN	ANGELO BADA
SID	GIULIO ROSSI
BELLO	VINCENZO RESCHIGLIAN
HARRY	PIETRO AUDISIO
JOE	GLENN HALL
HAPPY	ANTONIO PINI-CORSI
LARKENS	BERNARD BEGUE
BILLY, an Indian	GEORGES BOURGEOIS
WOWKLE, his Squaw	MARIE MATTFELD
JAKE WALLACE, a Minstrel	ANDREA DE SEGUROLA
JOSE CASTRO, with Ramerrez's Band	EDOARDO MISSIANO
THE PONY EXPRESS RIDER	LAMBERTO BELLERI

Men of the Camp and Boys of the Ridge.

CONDUCTOR . . . . ARTURO TOSCANINI
Stage Manager, JULES SPECK   Chorus Master, GIULIO SETTI   Technical Director, EDWARD SIEDLE

TIME—During the days of the gold fever—1849-1850   PLACE—Cloudy Mountain, California, a mining camp.

"In those strange days, people coming from—God knows where, joined forces in that far western land, and, according to the rude custom of the camp, their very names were soon lost and unrecorded, and here they struggled, laughed, gambled, cursed, killed, loved and worked out their strange destinies in a manner incredible to us of to-day. Of one thing only are we sure—they lived!"—*Early History of California.*

SYNOPSIS OF SCENERY
Act I.—The "Polka" saloon. At night.   Act II.—The home of Minnie. The same night
Act III.—The Redwood Forest. A week later.

The Mise en scene produced under the direction of Edward Siedel; Scenery by James Fox; Costumes by Madame Louise Musaeus; Lighting Effects by Frederick G. Gaus.

THE METROPOLITAN OPERA COMPANY
desires to make public acknowledgement of its indebtedness, and to express its cordial thanks to
MR. DAVID BELASCO
for his most valuable and kind assistance in the stage production of 'The Girl of the Golden West.'

Imagining that minstrel shows had guided Puccini's inspiration, the caricaturist Amerio Cagnoni drew Tito Ricordi, Vimercati, Puccini (with minstrel figures) and Gatti-Casazza at the "fiftieth curtain call" after the premiere of La Fanciulla. *Below left, cover design of the printed score, drawn from Blanche Bates' characterization in the original play; at right, Emmy* Destinn and Enrico Caruso at the Polka saloon in the first act. *Bottom left, with Pasquale Amato (right foregrown) as the haughty sheriff, Destinn poses with the nearly hanged Caruso to reenact the rescue scene of Act III. Caruso's sketch of the back of Puccini's head dates from the previous summer, when the Met performed at the Théâtre du Châtelet.*

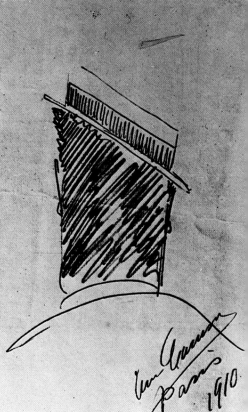

It was Tito Ricordi who in 1906 tried to arrange a collaboration between Gabriele D'Annunzio (facing page, top) and Puccini. The poet was living and working at the villa "La Versiliana" at Pietrasanta (below), not far from Torre del Lago. There were meetings and an exchange of letters. There was talk of Rose of Cyprus (letter at bottom left). Puccini did not conceal his perplexity and wrote to Tito, "Certainly D'Annunzio has his head in the clouds, but he has come down to earth in my direction, suffice it to say." Between the poet's delays and the composer's uncertainties, however, matters dragged on inconclusively. What Puccini did not find in the other man's work was directness of language or of dramatic situation.

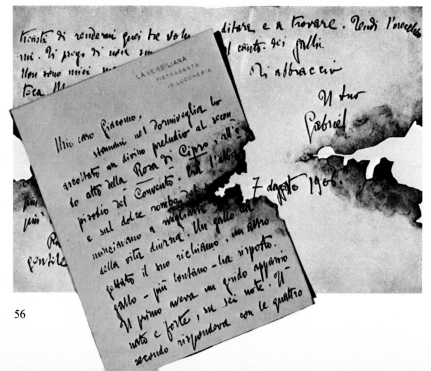

XXVII. IMPOSSIBLE COLLABORATION WITH D'ANNUNZIO

The following April (1907) the poet came to life again. Puccini to Tito: "D'Annunzio is making me offers again. This morning I got a letter saying 'The old nightingale has reawakened with spring and would like to sing for me.' " But this nightingale was not destined to sing. Other composers set D'Annunzio's plays to music in years to come—Mascagni (top of facing page), Zandonai (lower right, facing page), Pizzetti, Montemezzi—but with Puccini, as much as the poet devoutly wished for it, nothing ever worked out. Puccini tactfully said that D'Annunzio's lines were music in themselves and did not need his help. The poet felt rebuffed by this important composer—a blow to his considerable ego. Bottom, caricatures of the two.

As early as the first days of 1900, it had occurred to Puccini's publisher that the composer could collaborate with Gabriele D'Annunzio, the poet who had succeeded to Carducci's place in the affection and esteem of the Italians. Nothing came of it then, but during the period that ran from *Madama Butterfly,* so full of personal travails and artistic uncertainty, this scheme rose again, to the point of becoming more and more outlined and specific. It was Tito Ricordi who steered Puccini onto this path.

The two artists met in Versilia in 1906. Puccini confessed his own needs, his aspiration toward a higher form of human poetry, toward a deep self-renewal. The poet, after listening to him, proposed *Parisina,* a legend he had elaborated in the fashion of digging it out of "a poem in which life and dreams interact mysteriously, as they do in the soul of man." Puccini would take this proposal under consideration. Later, with great diplomacy, he replied that he could not feel it; thanks, but no thanks. A few months passed, and now D'Annunzio stepped forward with another plot, *La Rosa di Cipro* (The Rose of Cyprus). Puccini read it, talked it over with the poet and then wrote to Ricordi, "It's a rather romantic subject, a legend, a fable with a tragic ending. There is still correcting and discussion to be done, but it seems to me something that could be set to music and has strong dramatic interest." But this was a rose whose bloom would quickly fade: the project was discarded.

D'Annunzio persisted. Collaboration with Puccini interested him. He knew that if he worked with this composer, the royalties would be very generous. He tried to theorize with Puccini a sort of ideal collaboration between poetry and music. But each time he proposed subjects that did not possess a theatrical sense, with verses that were too far-out and precious. The fact was that these two great artists did not take the chance of making an alliance, at least as one human being to another, or of coming to an understanding on the aesthetic level. Puccini wanted something new, but not to intellectualize himself to the point of emptiness, and he could not make room for sterile aesthetic games. His crisis was an existential crisis on the one hand, but above all on the other a crisis of language. The meeting between D'Annunzio and Puccini would produce nothing.

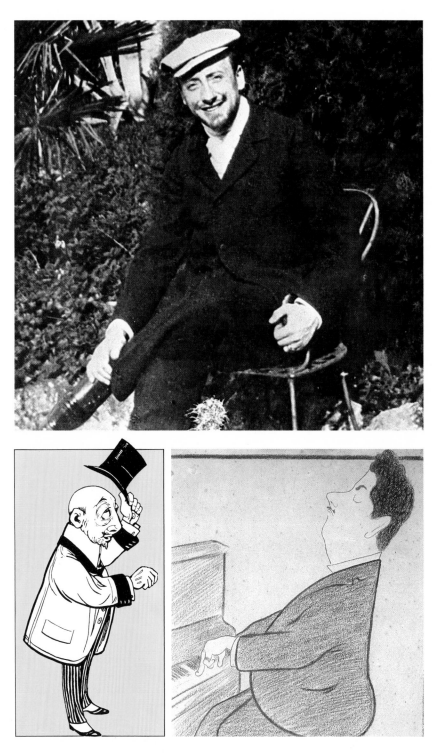

Puccini, who had established a mutual-admiration society with Franz Lehár, wanted to write a Viennese-style operetta, something light and different, but World War I intervened, so the scenario by two Viennese writers was reworked into an Italian opera libretto by Giuseppe Adami. La Rondine *reached the stage at Monte Carlo on March 28, 1917, with Gilda Dalla Rizza (below) and the elegant tenor Tito Schipa, Gino Marinuzzi conducting. Initial enthusiasm faded, however, with further performances. Below right, program of a 1919 revival in Monte Carlo and (bottom) the interior of the theater there. The score is expert, but its mixture of froth with heavier drama remains perplexing.*

XXVIII. STORY OF A SWALLOW

OPÉRA DE MONTE CARLO
Sous le Haut Patronage de
S. A. S. LE PRINCE DE MONACO
Direction RAOUL GUNSBOURG

Mardi 15 Avril 1919, en Soirée
à 8 heures un quart

LA RONDINE
(L'Hirondelle)

OPÉRA EN 3 ACTES. POÈME DE GIUSEPPE ADAMI
Musique de G. PUCCINI

Madge de Livry	...	Mme DELLA RIZZA
Lisette	...	MARCHINI
Yvette	...	LINDA
Souzi	...	KERLANE
Bianca	...	DUBOST
Ruggero	...	MM. TITO SCHIPA
Prunier	...	BONFANTI
Rambaldo	...	DELEUZE
Gobin	...	CH. DELMAS
Crébillon	...	STEPHAN
Périchot	...	PRAT
Un Étudiant	...	ECHÈNE
Le Majordome	...	MUNOL

Chef d'Orchestre : M. VICTOR DE SABATA

The world was turned on its head: the World War had broken out. It was the end of a society. The last sparks of the Belle Epoque were extinguished by a pistol shot at Sarajevo. And Puccini was even more in crisis, more alone, more desperate. Giulio Ricordi had died in 1912. For Puccini it was a terrible blow. He felt old, near the end of his life cycle as an artist. With Tito, the son of Giulio Ricordi, and with the entire publishing house, his relations had grown tense. Puccini did not wish to be considered a museum exhibit; he felt he had much more to say. But he knew too that to do so he needed encouragement and stimulation. Meanwhile, Tito Ricordi was urging him to resume negotiations with D'Annunzio. For the only time in his life, Puccini changed publishers. He had a project in mind: he wanted to set an operetta to music. On September 14, 1914, he wrote to Sybil, "*La Rondine* [The Swallow] is the title of the little opera that will be finished in the spring; it's a light work, sentimental and a little comical—sympathetic, clear, singing, with little waltzes, and with happy and touching tones." The librettist was an able young man, Giuseppe Adami, working from an original by two Viennese writers. Willing to do anything to please the Maestro, Adami worked with a will, though Puccini's mood was not the happiest. He had fought with Toscanini; he had changed publishers (only for one opera, to be sure, but it disturbed him none the less). In a letter he described himself "alone and sad as an elegy." Still, he continued to write music. His work was the one life preserver that kept him afloat.

In March 1917, *La Rondine* made its debut at Monte Carlo. Gino Marinuzzi conducted, with Gilda Dalla Rizza and Tito Schipa as principals. It was no longer a case of an operetta but of a real drama, in three acts. The story vaguely recalls that of *La Traviata*. It tells of a kept woman who, after a real romance with a young man, in order not to be a liability to his life and to society returns to being supported by a rich banker. The public was satisfied and applauded; the critics sang its praises. There is plenty of good music, plenty of ability in this *Rondine,* but there is also a grave defect, a big limitation: Puccini, as he well knew, was singing to himself. In some ways he was imitating himself.

Above, a scene from La Rondine *as produced in 1971 at the Teatro Comunale in Bologna. Left, Puccini with a niece of his and librettist Giuseppe Adami around the time of the premiere. True to his inner artistic voices, Puccini thought better of the work than the general opinion held of it, feeling he had realized his aims: "If the subject is nothing more than pleasant, it seems to me the music is worth more than that. I have drawn from the third act all the dramatic element it contains and arrived at the end with finesse, without shouting or orchestral bombast. Everything is in tune." Magda's two solos have remained popular, and in recent times* La Rondine *has come due for a number of successful revivals.*

Just before the outbreak of World War I, Puccini was staying in Paris and saw a one-act play that interested him, La Houppelande *by Didier Gold. A stark drama of dark coloration, with its tale of life and sudden death aboard a barge moored along the banks of the Seine, it offered a chance to move beyond the sentimental tone that had served him well in the past. Adapted as a libretto* by Giuseppe Adami, this became Il Tabarro *(The Cloak), first of the three short operas comprising* Il Trittico *(The Triptych), title page at right. The scene sketch below suggests the impressionistic local Parisian color that also attracted Puccini to the subject. This was the first time since* Le Villi *that the composer tried a short opera, though the form was a popular one.*

XXIX. THE TRIPTYCH

Il Tabarro *soon had the company of*
Suor Angelica *and* Gianni Schicchi;
*though different in color and accent,
all three deal with death, confinement
and a longing to escape.* Suor
Angelica *takes place in a sheltered
community of nuns, not too far
removed from the convent of Vico
Pelago (opposite page, lower left),
where the composer's sister was a
nun. Center picture below,* the opera as conceived for La Scala
in 1962 by Ardengo Soffici. The
third opera, Puccini's only comedy,
Gianni Schicchi, derived from an
episode in Dante's Inferno;
below, Gianni Vagnetti's 1959
La Scala design, and opposite page,
a sketch for the protagonist's
nightshirt. Bottom picture, Il
Tabarro designed by G. Miglioli
for the same 1959 La Scala version.

It was necessary to start again somehow, even if the social and historic climate was not the most propitious. The World War was claiming its victims on the fields of Europe, which was changing deeply; a certain type of society was dead, though no one yet admitted it. For Puccini there was only one way to change—by working. He read, he kept informed, he heard new music, new composers—Stravinsky, Webern, the atonal school. He did not let himself be led astray, but it seemed to enrich his experience, to give new stimulus to his search. He had never been a lazy man, and now even less. With Giovacchino Forzana and with Adami he was conceiving a new opus —three operas, each different from the others, one act apiece, to be presented in the same evening.

The first, to a French plot, is called *Il Tabarro* (The Cloak). It has deep, dark colors, rather in the manner of Zola. There is plenty of verism in it, but there is also a desperate, tragic hue—black, as it were—giving hints of something new. The second opera, *Suor Angelica,* takes place in a convent; the music is light, embroidered, airy, with the sweet melancholy of an early fall sunset. The third, *Gianni Schicchi,* is in fact the first and only example of a Puccini comic opera, perfect in inspiration, melodic invention and orchestration.

For *Il Tabarro* the labor was long; the other two he wrote in the twinkling of an eye, little more than a year. The premiere took place at the Metropolitan Opera in New York on December 14, 1918. The war had been over for a month and thirteen days. The public seemed pleased, the press perhaps more guarded. The year after, in 1919, at the Teatro Costanzi in Rome, the European premiere took place, and this time the success was genuine, but in Europe too the press remained cool. It was said and unsaid—one didn't have the nerve to come right out with it, because this was after all Puccini. But the novelty of the writing, the Maestro's desire to change his expressive style, was not fully digested. If the critics were to be believed, Puccini should limit himself to rewriting *La Bohème* and *Tosca.* He was sixty-one years old, but his heart still wanted to explore new paths. He had refined his orchestral technique enriched his vocabulary. Now all he needed was a a great new subject, so he could surpass himself.

Tito Ricordi (right) was the second in his family to bear that name: the first was his grandfather, sone of the Giò who founded the publishing house in 1808. Young Tito found himself with a great business inheritance from his father, Giulio, and this included the legacy of Puccini, whom Giulio had, so to speak, created. But Tito made the mistake of taking Puccini rather for granted, not understanding his anxieties and uncertainties, neglecting him in favor of younger composers—hoping to discover a new talent as his father had done. Below, the new factory that Tito built, later to be destroyed in World War II; bottom, the visit of King Umberto I to the plant, depicted by Adolf Hohenstein.

Tito Ricordi, who now headed the publishing firm, was the same age as Puccini. He was a handsome man who had tried to learn his father's business, but he was not a born publisher. One had to have a nose for it, the ability to indulge composers, the knowledge of how to step in discreetly, give counsel, mediate. Tito instead had a lot of presumption and ambition, a strong dose of snobbery—and the habit of not listening. He was quite familiar with Puccini, having made various trips with him, to London and Paris, on orders from Giulio, to help with important premieres in those capitals. For a while, after Tito became boss, the two understood each other. But then their relations grew tense to the breaking point. Till then, Tito had considered Puccini an asset, an inheritance. The Maestro had been a discovery of his father's and had always been published by Ricordi. As publisher, Tito wanted to find something new, something of his own. With that in mind he had started to focus on Riccardo Zandonai, much to Puccini's annoyance. Then too, Tito was not flexible: he did not understand the soul-searching, the anguish, the torment, the anxieties of Puccini's creative process. Besides, he fancied himself a stage director and was always having grandiose but not very stage-worthy ideas. And he was a society person, one who hung out in the intellectual salons of Milan, where it was beginning to be said that Puccini's petit-bourgeois sentimentality was no longer fashionable. It was Tito who had urged Puccini along the path of an impossible collaboration with D'Annunzio, and when the poet complained to him about the Maestro's never finalizing such a collaboration, Tito resented it, taking D'Annunzio's part. With *La Rondine* there was an open break.

Then, bit by bit, out of common interest, peace was restored between the two. But Puccini would never respect Tito and would never grant him the recognition of authority that had been Giulio Ricordi's. Relations between the two, even if affectionate, remained formal. Puccini never wholly trusted his new publisher, whom he criticized for an inability to make choices and offer guidance, to understand this peculiar art form known as the theater. And Tito, though he respected Puccini's popularity, never succeeded in grasping his greatness.

Despite their basic incompatibility, Tito and Puccini, who were the same age, had grown up together under Giulio Ricordi's tutelage and seemed to have a friendly enough relationship. It was Tito who accompanied Puccini to foreign cities for premieres, and they were frequently together socially, as in the yachting picture at bottom left and the rather guarded pose next to it, probably from one of their voyages. Below, in another Hohenstein design, the arrival of King Umberto I for his tour of inspection of the Ricordi factory—the sort of formal occasion on which the socially conscious Tito thrived, at the expense of his practical business sense. He lacked his father's shrewd psychology.

With the passage of time it is becoming more apparent that Puccini represented the swan song of romantic opera. Sensing the mood of the modern world, he built a musical bridge between the nineteenth and twentieth centuries, studying everything and everyone—Mahler, Bruckner, Mahler, Debussy, Schoenberg, Webern—assimilating, even anticipating the latest developments. His was a song of a changing Italy, in spite of that other part of Italy that did not change, or was slow to do so. Perhaps herein lies the real reason for his failed collaboration with D'Annunzio, the poet of grand illusions and quixotic dreams. Emotionally speaking, Puccini always remained a verist.

CONCERTO INTONA-RUMORI.

Gridando ed esclamando: — Dio, che fotta !
N'usciron tutti con la testa rotta ;

Alcuni pei rumor ch'avean inteso,
Ed altri pei cazzotti ch'avean preso!

TEATRO DAL VERME
Martedì 21 Aprile - Ore 21

GRAN CONCERTO
FUTURISTA
D'INTONARUMORI

Precederà
un discorso di MARINETTI

Esecuzione
delle 3 spirali di rumori intonati
composte e dirette da
LUIGI RUSSOLO

inventore dell'Arte dei Rumori:

1. Risveglio di una città.
2. Si pranza sulla terrazza del Kursaal.
3. Convegno d'aeroplani e d'automobili.

Orchestra di 18 intonarumori

3 rombatori	1 gorgogliatore
3 crepitatori	3 ululatori
2 scoppiatori	1 scrosciatore
3 stropicciatori	1 sibilatore
1 ronzatore	

Questi nuovissimi strumenti elettrici
furono inventati e costruiti
da LUIGI RUSSOLO e UGO PIATTI

Invitiamo il pubblico milanese ad ascoltare serenamente, senza ostilità preconcette, questo Concerto d'Intonarumori (nuova voluttà acustica armoniosa, non cacofonica) di cui gli è riservata la primizia.

DIREZIONE DEL MOVIMENTO FUTURISTA: Corso Venezia, 61 - MILANO

MUSICA FUTURISTA DI BALILLA PRATELLA

BOCCIONI

XXXI. THE LURE OF THE AVANT-GARDE

Opposite page, top: caricature of the "Grand Futurist Concert of Noise Intoners" given by Luigi Russolo and Ugo Piatti at the Teatro Dal Verme in 1913 with the blessings of Filippo Tommaso Marinetti, father of Futurism; far left, poster for the concert and title page designed by Umberto Boccioni for a book confidently entitled Futurist Music. *by Balilla Pratella. On this page: caricature of Wagner, founder of "music of the future"; page from the score* Il Risveglio di una Città (A City Awakens) *by Russolo; and Boccioni's painting* Riot in the Gallery. *A logical outgrowth of industrialization, the futurist concerts did in fact provoke riots.*

He would never make it wholly understood, or even admit it to his friends, but Puccini was always hungry for the new. His musical gifts were substantial, his fund of melody was nearly inexhaustible, but that was not enough for him. Even since Giulio Ricordi sent him to Bayreuth to study the operas of Wagner, after the half-success of *Edgar,* Puccini had remained fascinated by the endless possibilities of music, by its colors, its harmonies, its expressive potential. He had never stopped trying to illuminate these possibilites. Whenever he found himself in a strange city, the two things he did first were to go to the theater (whether or not he understood the language)—to see new scenic solutions, to look for plots—and to hear new music. In Paris he discovered Debussy. In Vienna he discovered Schoenberg and Webern, studied Mahler and Bruckner, got interested in atonality. In New York he was taken by the rhythms and cadences of jazz. Back in Paris, he went to hear Stravinsky.

He didn't copy—he observed carefully. Therefore, many times it was he who anticipated the more modern composers. He was no imitator, but he absorbed new expressive means, to see if they would work for him, if they would enrich his extraordinary capacity of writing music by way of telling a story. He knew that the more the years passed, the more the twentieth century proceeded, the more difficult it would be to write opera. He even perceived that opera, as he knew it, was becoming an obsolete form. Speaking of *La Fanciulla del West* he affirmed, "But how hard it is to write opera today!" It was a sentence dropped in a letter, but how much it had to say about his extraordinary sensitivity to the times in which he lived. Puccini sensed a crisis in the artistic climate, but he didn't give in to it. He knew that if he developed his own capacities, perhaps he could give this art form a last masterpiece, his swan song. For this he was insatiable; for this he didn't hesitate to put himself up against composers less well known than he, albeit much less open in their expression, but who evidenced a torment, an anziety for renewal and for new expressiveness, which was also his desire. He never theorized or proclaimed. The only way he knew how to resolve his questions was with work. Because as Toscanini insisted, music is knowing how to sing—having the desperate gift of song to share.

Puccini's tormented search for librettos suited to his artistic nature led, toward the end of his life, to the idea of an opera on the exotic fable Turandot *by Carlo Gozzi, whose picture appears at the extreme right of the facing page. Gozzi, an opponent of the naturalism of Goldoni, was a pro-aristocratic satirist—an unlikely bedfellow for Puccini—*

but the librettists, Adami and Simoni, romanticized the play, following Friedrich Schiller's nineteenth-century German translation of it. Simoni, author of light comedies in Venetian dialect, and Adami, the versifier, argued with Puccini about the number of acts: they wanted three, he at first wanted two. But the project moved ahead.

XXXII. THE LONG GESTATION OF "TURANDOT"

It was toward the end of 1919 that Puccini began to think about writing an opera based on the fable of Count Carlo Gozzi about the cruel Chinese princess Turandot. Carlo Clausetti and Renzo Valcarenghi, who had replaced Titio Ricordi in the management of the publishing house, allied themselves with Giuseppe Adami, in collaboration with Renato Simoni—theater critic of *Il Corriere della Sera,* an author of plays, a talented stage director and a man of wide cultivation. Simoni had Puccini read the play *Turandot,* and the composer wrote to him, "To exalt the passion of Turandot, who for so long has suffocated in the ashes of her great pride . . . When all's said, I cling to the feeling that *Turandot* is the least bizarre and most human of Gozzi's theater pieces." So another work began. Puccini immersed himself in it with a tenacious and desperate will. He gave no more orders, didn't impose his will on his librettists, though he did exhort them to do a quick and good job, to get on with it. And somehow he sensed, darkly but surely, that he was near the end. The Maestro suffered from diabetes and depression. He tired easily, sometimes thinking he had bungled the choice of libretto and subject. Then he would pull himself together. When they sent him an act, he would set it to music with a will and great inspiration—and also relapses of doubt. Was the music too advanced?

The support of Toscanini's judgment (they had made peace again) was a comfort to him. But the problem of the finale tormented him. He wasn't sure whether the opera should be in two or three acts, discussing this at length with Adami and Simoni. He felt the turning point of the drama should be the death of Liù, a death that could "exert a force toward the thawing of the princess." What concerned him most, however, was the final duet between the princess, in love at last, and Prince Calaf. It was a duet that by Puccini's own description should be "the key—but it should have something about it of the grand, the bold, the unexpected, and not leave things where they began." Again, in a letter to Adami: "The duet, the duet! Everything beautiful, decisive, theatrically alive is in it!" In the composer's mind this duet had to represent the triumph of love over everything—over cruelty, over death. It was a song that he, who had always dreamed of love, would not be able to finish.

Puccini's travails during the composition of Turandot *produced many a letter, such as the one shown here (center) to Simoni. At the piano (opposite page) that remains today in the Puccini Foundation museum at Lucca— the same piano that appears in his late photo at bottom left —Puccini created the immortal melodies of Calàf, Liù and the* frigid princess. *In spite of crises of faith, suggestions of quitting and the sickness that lodged in Puccini's throat,* Turandot *(libretto cover design at left) continued to take shape. The Maestro's death cut it short, leaving behind a clutch of sketches, like the one at bottom right, for the difficult final duet of the opera.*

The Maestro's strong constitution gradually gave way before the onslaught of a cancerous tumor in his throat. Toward the end of 1924 he went to Brussels under the care of Prof. Ledoux at the Institut de la Couronne. To the faithful Adami he wrote, "Caro Adamino, here I am. Poor me! They say I'll be here six weeks. This is unwanted. And

Turandot?" Though the treatment seemed to augur well, Puccini died of heart failure soon after. Below, portrait of the Maestro by Luigi de' Servi; at right, two dramatic documents of the composer's last days. Top, a note (he could not talk) asking for cold water; below, his last letter, addressed to Giuseppe Adami, his librettist.

XXXIII. THE END

Puccini died at four in the morning on November 29, 1924. Beside his bed lay the last pages of the Turandot *manuscript, including the sketches for the finale, depicting the triumph of love over human cruelty. The world was shaken by the news. As a mark of respect, La Scala canceled its performance of Boito's* Nerone *(poster at*

right). There was a funeral procession in Brussels (upper left) and, several days later, further honors followed in Milan (bottom). On the second anniversary of his death, the Maestro's remains were transferred to a new burial site in the chapel of his former villa at Torre del Lago, where a memorial now stands.

It was toward the end of 1923 that the Maestro began to complain of a bad cough and a persistent, stinging, bothersome sore throat. At first, in view of the fact that he had had a smoker's cough throughout his career, he did not make too much of it. But when it didn't clear up, he visited his doctor and a specialist in Milan, who could not find anything conclusive.

At the end of June 1924 he was back in Viareggio, where he spent the summer trying to finish that damned *Turandot* duet, which did not come to him as readily as he wanted. In September, Toscanini, as artistic director of La Scala, visited Puccini to settle the date and particulars concerning the premiere of *Turandot,* which was scheduled for 1925. They spoke of the famous duet, which Puccini affirmed "I have made into an elephant's head." After a month Puccini had to go back to Milan and face La Scala. He called Adami and Simoni together, and they all went to Toscanini, with whom they reviewed the whole opera, plus the sketches for the duet. The conductor was impressed by two things—the music, and the appearance of the composer, who seemed tired, old, weak. In mid-October, Puccini went to Florence, where he underwent more thorough diagnosis. The outcome was ominous: cancer of the throat. Naturally this verdict was partially concealed from Puccini, who wrote to Adami, "I'm going to Brussels to see a famous specialist. I'm leaving right away. Will they operate? Will it kill me or cure me? So I can't go any farther, and there is *Turandot*. . ."

He left on November 4, accompanied by his son Tonio and by Clausetti. He had the sketches for the final duet with him. During the trip he felt very sick. He went into the clinic on the 7th. There he was started on radium treatments. The morning of the 24th, full-scale treatment began: his throat was pierced by seven crystal radiation needles, inserted directly into the tumor. The operation lasted three hours and forty minutes, with only local anesthetic, so as not to place undue strain on the patient's heart. The sick man could no longer speak and had to write his needs on a pad. For three days he seemed to be recovering, to the point where Dr. Ledoux permitted himself cautious optimism: "Puccini will pull through." But on the 28th he had a heart attack, and he died the next morning.

Turandot, *Puccini's most ambitious dream, was left unfinished. The Maestro had already shown Arturo Toscanini his ideas about how the finale would go. It was Toscanini who suggested to the publisher Ricordi that another composer, Franco Alfano (upper right), be entrusted with completing the score from Puccini's sketches. The opera reached the stage on an emotional evening in 1926 at the Teatro alla Scala. At the premiere (poster, upper left), as a mark of respect for the composer, the performance was left unfinished. In subsequent performances, Alfano's completion was performed. Alfano had done a modest, workmanlike job, for which he sought no recognition on his own. But Toscanini had misgivings about it.*

XXXIV. THE PREMIERE OF "TURANDOT"

April 25, 1926. Seventeen months had passed since the Maestro's death. At Toscanini's suggestion, the House of Ricordi had entrusted to Franco Alfano—himself the composer of several operas— the task of completing *Turandot,* working from the sketches Puccini had left. The time for the premiere had arrived. Mussolini had announced he would be there and ordered the fascist hymn played before the performance; Toscanini refused to conduct it, so the Duce did not appear at La Scala. But the theater was packed with important people. At exactly nine o'clock, Toscanini sounded the first notes. Turandot, Liù and Calaf were sung by Rosa Raisa, Maria Zamboni and Miguel Fleta, with Raisa's husband, the baritone Giacomo Rimini, as Ping and Carlo Walter as Timur. The first act had a clamorous success, the second a little less so. When it came to Act III, there was intense applause after "Nessun dorma" and "Tu che di gel sei cinta." After the death of Liù, the chorus sang, "Liù, goodness, Liù, gentleness, sleep! Forget! Liù, poetry!" At this point Toscanini brought the orchestra to a halt, then turned slowly to the great auditorium. With a voice moved by emotion, he said hoarsely, "Here the opera ends, because at this point the Maestro died." That evening *Turandot* ended—unfinished, as Puccini left it—with the words of Toscanini.

The next day the pontiffs of the press were more illuminating than usual. But they showed they had understood neither Puccini's underlying personality nor the importance of *Turandot.* A long time would be required before the critics would recognize the true worth not only of this opera but of all Puccini's music. *Turandot* was without doubt its composer's most ambitious dream, the opera over which he had spent himself the most, over which he had suffered the most, in which he expressed the changes that had arisen in the course of his life as man and artist. Intense, suffused with an unreal, magical atmosphere, full of new colors and spiced rhythms and phrases of strong profile, *Turandot* remains the ultimate romantic opera of the twentieth century. With it ended the heyday of Italian art, of a whole climate, a whole vocabulary. This is just why the climactic duet was not completed by Puccini. This last romantic opera in history should not have an ending.

After its premiere in 1926,
Turandot *enjoyed a triumph on
all the major stages of the world.
Below right, two sketches by
Brunelleschi for the first La
Scala production; at left, Cecil
Beaton's design for the Metropolitan
Opera in 1961, with Birgit
Nilsson as the protagonist,
challenging Franco Corelli with
her riddles in Act II; bottom*
*of opposite page, a La Scala
production in recent years with
designs by Pier Luigi Pizzi.
This opera distances itself
from the bourgeois audience,
to whom Puccini's romantic operas
were so dear. Novelty of form,
dramatic intensity and
grand conception mark his
ultimate work. His orchestration
too was ambitiously modern.*

The same thing that happened with Verdi around the 1940s seems to be happening with Puccini today. He is no longer considered just a happy inventor of sweet melodies, a creature of fragile feminine figures. He is coming to be considered, rather, a true and very great musician. Studies of his work, and new productions of his operas, are multiplying.

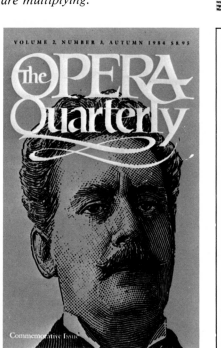

XXXV. PUCCINI TODAY

Beloved and performed in Italy, Puccini abroad is outright idolized. He is considered perhaps the most Italian of Italian composers. The critical revaluation of him keeps growing: books about him, study seminars, festivals, testimonials, symposiums make him an artist for our time. Opposite page, top: a collage of recent articles about Puccini; *below it, a festival poster; at left (top) the cover of an American periodical with a monograph on Puccini, and (bottom) a whole page of a daily paper dedicated to the opening of a La Scala season with* Turandot. *Below, a view of Franco Zeffirelli's 1983-84* Turandot, *Act II, Scene 2, La Scala production, publicized at bottom left of facing page.*

Puccini is perhaps the composer most beloved and familiar to aficionados of romantic opera. His is a broad public, unlimited by language, age or fashion. It is no coincidence that among the most frequently recorded operas are two of his, *La Bohème* and *Madama Butterfly.* Being so justly popular and enjoying such public favor, this composer has been slow to attract the serious attention of critics. In all the years since his death, Puccini has been judged, especially in Italy, a too simple and facile composer, the modest singer of little stories of love and death. Perhaps this meager luck with the critics stems from the fact that the Tuscan composer, who knew this craft as few others did, who had a genius for melody and expressed in his orchestration all the subtle shadings of our turbulent times, also knew how to move people, to speak directly to the heart of the listener and, as a young Italian critic, Lorenzo Arrugo, has said, to "make music cry." When we hear *La Bohème,* we feel with Mimi that our youth is not going to last.

Nowadays, as it happens, Puccini is considered not only a major composer but a foremost exponent of his own time, comparable to Schoenberg and Stravinsky, certainly of more secure standing than many contemporaries who drew more attention but have been forgotten by the public. This is owing in part to the work of several top-ranking conductors. Starting with Toscanini, then Gino Marinuzzi and Victor De Sabata, who during the 1950s gave a series of memorable performances at La Scala that revealed to students of music with what consistency, with what subtlety of color and variety of impressions, the master's art was informed. Following De Sabata's example, in our time came Herbert von Karajan's poetic interpretations of *La Bohème* and *Tosca,* of *Turandot* and *Madama Butterfly.* And after Karajan have come such exponents as Carlos Kleiber, Georges Prêtre and James Levine, showing the wide range and richness of Puccini's timbres.

To interpreters of this magnitude we owe the joy of having revealed to us the full scope of Puccini's achievement, of having restored it, refurbished, from ready charges of facile formula, and of helping us understand that with Puccini we are in the presence of a great composer of our past, present and future.

Top picture: Heinrich Conried at his desk in the general manager's office at the Metropolitan Opera House; a shrewd showman, he invited Puccini to New York as the composer's popularity was rising. Middle picture: Puccini poses on the Auguste Viktoria *with his publisher, Giulio Ricordi, who came to bid him bon voyage, solicitous as always.*

Bottom, starring in Manon Lescaut *in its first Met production in 1907 were the glamorous Lina Cavalieri, a* femme fatale *offstage as well as on, and the best-loved tenor in the history of the company, Enrico Caruso. Many of their countrymen attended their performances, thanks to a recent and unprecedented wave of immigration to the New World.*

POSTSCRIPT: PUCCINI IN AMERICA

by Mary Jane Phillips Matz

In 1906, riding confidently on his European and South American successes, Puccini was invited to New York by Heinrich Conried, manager of the Metropolitan Opera. Knowing that Conried had at his disposal artists of the caliber of Enrico Caruso, Geraldine Farrar, Lina Cavalieri, Louise Homer and Antonio Scotti, Puccini was happy to accept. Almost fifty and world-famous, he embarked on the *Kaiserin Auguste Viktoria*, having first bought a fur-lined coat, "because it is very cold in New York." Anticipating his wife's seasickness, he had engaged "a cabin amidships and a vomitorium for Elvira," who lived up to his expectations and became ill.

An unforeseen problem was fog off Sandy Hook: for two days the ship lay at anchor almost within reach of New York. January 17 came and went, and with it the dress rehearsal of *Manon Lescaut*, which Puccini's lucrative six-week contract provided he should "supervise." On the 18th, the day of the first performance, the ship was fogbound between quarantine and Hoboken. At the last moment the fog lifted, and the *Auguste Viktoria* docked at her pier in the Hudson River. An official welcoming party and a horde of reporters, there since early morning, rushed to receive Puccini, who surprised them by announcing he was fascinated by the American Far West and might write an opera about it. He spoke of Bret Harte and David Belasco, while the press took his measure: "Very different from some of the Italian maestros who have visited New York." Tall, robust, tanned from years of hunting and roaming the marshland, he was clean-shaven, save for his jaunty moustache, and wore fine tailored clothes, exuding a self-confidence that betrayed nothing of the essentially shy man within. Rich and sure of himself, he was everything the public would want this celebrated composer to be.

Puccini left the ship at six o'clock. At seven he was dining in his suite at the Astor Hotel. At eight he arrived at the opera house with his frock coat folded in a small valise. After a quick change, he took his seat in the manager's box. *Manon Lescaut* was already well into its first act. When the lights went up, the audience's reaction to seeing

At left, a caricature by Caruso's own hand shows Cavalieri arguing at rehearsal with Antonio Scotti, who sang Lescaut in the performance. In the years since then, Puccini's opera has been revived sporadically. Directly below, Mirella Freni in Act II with Ermanno Mauro during the 1984-85 season, pleading for her lover's forgiveness.

At bottom, two versions of Manon Lescaut's poignant death scene: left, Renata Scotto with Plácido Domingo, the versatile tenor who soon afterward conducted La Bohème at the Met. On the right, a production of two decades earlier shows two other famous performers, Richard Tucker and Renata Tebaldi, in the roles of Manon and Des Grieux.

A panorama of Madama Butterfly *at the Met. Opposite page, far left: Geraldine Farrar was the first to sing the protagonist there, loved by the public, more guardedly admired by Puccini. Next to her, a celebrated Butterfly of later years, Licia Albanese, who revived the work after it had lain dormant during World War II. Below them, the 1958 stage design by Motohiro Nagasaka, who brought Japanese authenticity to the architecture and locale. Near left, Caruso's sketch of Maestro Arturo Vigna, whose conducting Puccini found distinctly routine. Directly below, Renata Scotto in one of Cio-Cio San's happier moments —among the soprano's many Puccini characterizations at the Met.*

him for the first time, one of near-hysteria, left the composer astonished. "I had to take six bows from the manager's box after the first act!" he reported to his publisher the next day. "After the second act, I took seven curtain calls onstage. After the third . . . I just remained in the manager's box, applauding the artists while the audience shouted and cheered. After the last act, more acclaim, four bows. Cavalieri was truly very fine; I was truly struck by her temperament, especially in the spiritual and emotional moments. . . . Caruso is the usual, extraordinary Des Grieux. Scotti is very good."

When *Madama Butterfly* went into rehearsal, Puccini had the chance to honor his contract. He was overworked, he said. The rehearsals were all too hurried. He had to arrange all the rehearsal himself and blamed Eugène Dufriche, the stage manager, for taking advantage of him. Of the conductor, Arturo Vigna, he said, "His orchestra does not obey him." Caruso and Scotti had already sung *Madama Butterfly* at other theaters, but for Geraldine Farrar, as for the Metropolitan, this was the first time. Puccini, disconcerted by her habit of "marking" (singing less than full-voice at rehearsals), was disappointed: she sang off-key, he said, forced her voice and could not be heard in the farthest reaches of the house. Of Caruso the composer complained he was "lazy" and "won't learn anything . . . he is too self-satisfied."

At the dress rehearsal, there was pandemonium, the house overflowing. People brought sandwiches, Farrar said, and "that new fad, the thermos bottle." Puccini had never in his life seen anything like that disorderly crew. "Nobody knew anything," he complained, having fought for an extra final rehearsal. Still, by his own account, the first performance "went very well as far as the press and public

On this page, three famous singers who made their Met debuts in La Bohème. *Luciano Pavarotti, directly below, first played Rodolfo there in November 1968, following in the footsteps of Jussi* Bjoerling, *a* Bohème *debutant of 1938. At bottom, Grace Moore, who introduced her Mimì in 1938 and later filmed it; her protégée Dorothy Kirsten, who stepped into her shoes in 1945.*

are concerned, though not for me. . . .The press was unanimous in its approval."

Lionized by New Yorkers, he attended many social events and went sightseeing like any other tourist. He hoped to see "Niagara Fall" and went to "China Twon" (sic). Caruso, who also lived at the Astor, would round up Scotti and other cronies so the clan could explore the city together. A frequent destination was Little Italy, where they joined Marziale Sisca, publisher of the Italian-language newspaper *La Follia di New York*, at Del Pezzo's restaurant, where they ate and played poker and *scopa*. Puccini also went to plays, vaudeville performances and minstrel shows. Searching for a new subject for his next opera, he saw three David Belasco plays — *The Music Master*, *The Rose of the Rancho* and *The Girl of the Golden West*, which was playing to full houses at the Belasco Theater. The star was Blanche Bates, for whom Belasco had also written *Madame Butterfly*. Fascinated by the American West, Puccini had seen Buffalo Bill Cody in Milan in 1890. "I enjoyed the show," he wrote his brother at that time. "Buffalo Bill and his troupe are a company of North Americans with some Red Indians and buffaloes. They perform magnificent feats of shooting and give realistic presentations of scenes that have taken place on the frontier. In eleven days they took in 120,000 lire at the box office!"

Now, seeing *The Girl of the Golden West* at the Belasco, Puccini was captivated by the atmospheric settings, which included a moving curtain-panorama of the Cloudy Mountains of California, with the heroine's cabin, and a blizzard that required thirty-two stagehands with wind and snow machines. The musical local color too was irresistible: from the Polka saloon echoed a black song from the South; there was an authentic California minstrel band with a singer, concertina, banjo and xylophone, which played such Americana as "Pop Goes the Weasel," "Coal Oil Tommy" and "Rosalie, the Prairie Flower." Belasco recorded for posterity that when the minstrel appeared in the first act to sing "Old Dog Tray," Puccini exclaimed, "Ah, there's my theme at last!" (This last anecdote gave rise to considerable misunderstanding among European musicologists, who assume to this day that Puccini used Stephen Foster songs in his opera. Though he took fragments from Foster's words, Puccini's melodies were his own.)

Within weeks, he was asking Belasco for a copy of the play. By July, he had firmly decided to compose the opera and was getting popular music of the Gold Rush period sent to him, together with "authentic Red Indian songs," to absorb their style and feeling. Translation was entrusted to Carlo Zangarini — astonishingly, the son of a Colorado woman. Puccini had his own clear idea of how to create the final act: the mountains, the forest, Minnie pleading for Ramerrez' life, his release and "the great love duet as they move slowly away, and a scene of grief and desolation among the cowboys." (The composer had not yet grasped the fact that there were no cowboys among the California

Figures of power: left, Giulio Gatti-Casazza, beginning a long tenure as general manager under the aegis of Met board chairman Otto H. Kahn (right), a tycoon who loved opera. Bottom, the dapper Puccini poses with Arturo Toscanini for Lionel Mapleson's candid camera during the Met's Paris tour, Théâtre du Châtelet, 1910—months before Puccini's second U.S. visit for Fanciulla.

Embarking in 1910, Puccini posed on board the Washington *with a ship's officer, Giulio Ricordi and the publisher's son, Tito, looking at the score of* La Fanciulla del West—*a new departure musically as well. Right, David Belasco in his studio, a genius of the realistic theater and source of two Puccini operas.*

Though infrequently revived by the Met after its premiere, La Fanciulla del West *came back with a bang in the 1961-62 season. Bottom, at the tense climax of Act II, Minnie (Dorothy Kirsten) plays poker with Sheriff Jack Rance (Anselmo Colzani) for top stakes—the life of the wounded Ramerrez, slumped on table.*

gold miners.)

It was inevitable that the world premiere would be given at the Metropolitan. By 1910 the company had a new manager, Giulio Gatti-Casazza, who had been enticed away from La Scala by Otto Kahn, chairman of the Met's board of directors. Kahn had also persuaded Gatti-Casazza to lure Arturo Toscanini away from La Scala with him. So Puccini could count on these two, plus Caruso and Pasquale Amato, for his new opera. "How happy I am with *The Girl*!" he exclaimed. "How I adore the subject!" But he had scarcely started work when his life was thrown into turmoil by the death of his housemaid Doria Manfredi, hounded to suicide by the composer's insanely jealous wife. In October 1908, when Elvira Puccini had driven Doria from the house, he lamented, "*The Girl* has completely dried up." After Doria's death in January and the ensuing legal melee, Puccini, separated from his wife, eventually agreed, in a supreme act of charity, to resume life with her, and by August 1909 he could write, "I am a little quieter now, and am working." By November he had "got to the third act." And in August 1910 he exulted, "So *The Girl* is finished at last!!" In November he again sailed for America, this time accompanied by his son and his publisher's son. He was given the imperial suite on the luxury liner *George Washington* and treated like royalty. For the Metropolitan Opera production, which Gatti-Casazza regarded as the most important event in the company's history, the enigmatic, fascinating David Belasco — "The Bishop of Broadway" (he affected a clerical collar), one of the most skilled showmen of all time — was in charge of the staging and of making the singers act. Puccini was to oversee the production; he even got the eight horses he wanted onstage. Public curiosity was stimulated by Gatti-Casazza's decision to double the ticket prices for opening night. And scalpers were said to be getting up to thirty times as much.

"Rehearsals are going very well," Puccini wrote home. "The opera is coming out splendidly — the first act a little long [he made some cuts], but the second magnificent and the third grandiose. Caruso is magnificent in his part, Destinn not bad, but she needs more energy. Toscanini — *the zenith, kind, good, adorable.* In short, I'm happy with my work, and I hope for the best. But how tremendously difficult is this work and this staging!"

The outcome was a triumph unlike any the composer had ever seen. In a cable he reported fifty-five curtain calls. The next day's headlines read "Riots over Puccini" and "America Proud of *The Girl of the Golden West* — a $20,000 House." Ernest De Weerth, a musicologist who was in the theater, recalled that "Toscanini carried every listener straight out of reality and into the world of fantasy." Of Caruso one critic wrote simply, "Ye gods, how he sang!" In the midst of tumultuous acclaim after the final curtain, Gatti-Casazza crowned Puccini with a silver wreath.

America had brought Puccini the fulfillment of his cherished dream of seeing his works staged with the care

For the world premiere in 1910, the publicity-conscious Met management spared no expense to make La Fanciulla del West *a historic event. To portray Ramerrez (alias Dick Johnson), the frontiersman forced to turn bandit by his father's death, no less than Enrico Caruso, photographed by Mishkin in his Western finery.*

Belasco did his best to coach convincing performances from Caruso, who had a mind of his own; from the noble-voiced but rather static Emmy Destinn (bottom) as Minnie, the Czech soprano who had sung Aida for Toscanini's Met debut; and from the baritone Pasquale Amato, who played Sheriff Rance.

When Arturo Toscanini came to the Metropolitan Opera for the first time in 1908, one of the novelties he introduced was Le Villi, *Puccini's short first opera, on a double bill with Mascagni's Cavalleria Rusticana. Below, Frances Alda, Australian-born wife of general manager Gatti-Casazza, in costume for Act II of* Le Villi, *in which she played Anna.*

After the success of La Fanciulla del West, *the Met asked Puccini for another world premiere—Il Trittico (The Triptych)—but World War I delayed the event until late 1918 and prevented the composer from returning. Left, a 1976 revival with Philip Booth, Renata Scotto and Lili Chookasian in* Il Tabarro, *first of the trio of contrasting one-act operas.*

and honor they required. The material rewards were great as well. After a dinner and reception at the Vanderbilt mansion, he was approached by a famous banker who asked how much he would charge for an autograph of Musetta's waltz from *La Bohème*. In a showroom window Puccini had seen a motor launch he wanted, so he named — and got — its price. From production royalties he received 120,000 lire, more than 1,600 times the sum his widowed mother had received each year to raise her family.

As fate would have it, this was Puccini's last trip to America. He might have come a third time in 1918 for the world premiere of *Il Trittico*, but it fell only a month after the Armistice, and ship's passage was not to be had. By visiting when he did, in 1907 and 1910, Puccini accomplished more than just generating publicity. By establishing his operas at the Metropolitan with his own artistic signature, he guaranteed a certain authenticity and

In the 1918 world premiere, the stars of Il Tabarro *were Luigi Montesanto, Claudia Muzio and Giulio Crimi, grouped at left. For* Suor Angelica, *second of the trilogy, Geraldine Farrar appeared as the gentle nun of the title (left below), while for the third,* Gianni Schicchi, *baritone Giuseppe De Luca played the Florentine (below right).*

"The afternoon off of a genius" *was one critic's characterization of* La Rondine (The Swallow) *when it flew in for a brief visit at the Met in the 1927-28 season, starring the beloved Lucrezia Bori and the honey-voiced tenor Beniamino Gigli (bottom). Left center, program for the first New York performance, a decade after the world premiere.*

founded a tradition that would endure long after his death. His operas have, in fact, remained among the most popular in the United States. And their appeal reaches beyond the confines of the opera stage. In the winter of 1984, a hit record on the rock-music market was Malcolm McLaren's *Madam Butterfly,* on which a soprano voice intones Puccini's "Un bel dì vedremo" in Italian against McLaren's driving beat and English lyrics, with the voices of Butterfly and Pinkerton explaining their predicaments. A chorus from *Turandot* is also on the record. So, nearly eighty years after Puccini came to teach the Metropolitan Opera public his own version of "her tale of woe," the rock public has again turned Butterfly's plaint into a hit. On the rock disc, the chorus raps "He'll be back" as Butterfly affirms, "I have faith in this love track." Once again, a fresh, raw passion for Puccini's music on the American scene proves the durability and universality of his appeal. Puccini is as viable today as he was in his own time.

EPILOGUE: PUCCINI THE ARTIST

by John W. Freeman

Puccini was that extreme rarity among composers, a talent purely of the theater. Unlike the other major opera composers — Monteverdi, Gluck, Mozart, Wagner, Rossini, Verdi, Strauss — he is unknown in the concert hall. His songs and instrumental compositions are few and negligible. Though he lived in a time when there was considerable pressure on Italian composers to dignify their art, to produce something more than entertainment, he had the gift of seeing himself as he was — a man born to write only for the stage.

Part of a stage composer's armory is his knowledge of the singing voice, and in this Puccini was again fortunate. Unlike his teacher Ponchielli and his contemporaries Leoncavallo and Mascagni, Puccini wrote naturally for the voice, without straining its capacity or unduly

LEONCAVALLO.

"I wish winter would last forever," sing the forlorn lovers in Act III of La Bohème, agreeing after Mimi's "Addio senza rancor" (left) not to part until spring. The opera's youthful poetry is distilled in Franco Zeffirelli's designs for the Metropolitan Opera 1981 production, which also shows the bleakness and poverty of the young people's world. The same French novel, Henry Mürger's Scènes de la Vie de Bohème, was set to music by Ruggero Leoncavallo (bottom left); other contemporaries of the verismo movement were Pietro Mascagni (directly below), Puccini's sometime student roommate, and Umberto Giordano (bottom), who wrote the popular French Revolutionary opera Andrea Chénier.

exploiting it. From the examples of Bellini, Donizetti and Verdi he learned the art of writing recitative and dialogue that flowed easily, introducing flights of melody where they would intensify the dramatic situation (never for their own sake). And when he came to the melodic set pieces, which are basically moments of repose in the dramatic structure, he used melody of a uniquely personal, character — what has come to be known as "Puccinian melody." He could do no wrong in writing for the voice. In this he differs from the younger colleagues whose work intermingled with his as the first two decades of the twentieth century progressed — Zandonai, Montemezzi, Respighi, Pizzetti. In their operas the vocal line is often arbitrarily constructed to fit some interesting sequence of harmonies in the orchestra. Being Italians by heritage as well as "moderns" by circumstance, they could not resist writing melody too, but it lacked the spontaneity of Puccini's. Often, listening to melodies like "Recondita armonia" or the love duet from the first act of Tosca, we have almost the feeling of hearing folk songs, pre-existing melodies that Puccini picked out of the air. And the sixth-chords of La Bohème became such a standard device of

Puccini's fame, bolstered by the powerful publicity of his publisher, Ricordi, tended to put rival composers in the shade. In fact their contributions to the dying era of Italian lyric art were important. The scholarly, discreetly modern Ildebrando Pizzetti (below) at first disdained opera, then tried to elevate it with classical and Biblical subjects. Italo Montemezzi (right) made his fame by setting a very literary melodrama, L'Amore di Tre Re by Sem Benelli, to music of refinement and passion. Neither equaled Puccini's melodic flow or the power of such a scene as the Tosca Te Deum (bottom, with Cornell MacNeil as Scarpia, in Franco Zeffirelli's 1985 Metropolitan production).

popular-song writers up through the 1940s that we tend to forget it was Puccini who influenced them, rather than the other way around.

Puccini shared with two other giants of twentieth-century opera, Richard Strauss and Leoš Janáček, the knack of writing phrases that would always be instantly recognizable as his. In that respect, their resemblance to folk or popular song ceased. Part of this knack is simply an inborn gift for melody — a gift that some composers (say, Prokofiev or Gershwin) possessed in abundance while others (say, Stravinsky or Bartók) did not. But while prodigal melody is helpful in writing an opera — most of the lasting operas have plenty of good tunes — it is not enough, nor is it any guarantee. The composer also needs a sense of prosody, the ability to weigh words and accents. And above all he must have a sixth sense for the stage. So, regardless of Puccini's distinction as a melodist, it is not for this alone that his operas succeeded. He also knew when to stop. His melodies never go on too long; in fact, they usually leave the listener wanting more. And they never appear at inappropriate moments. Sometimes Puccini used them as leitmotifs — tags to identify a character, a feeling. This idea gained currency through Wagner, but Puccini used it less literally, as Strauss did, to suggest rather than denote. For all the tuneful flow of the second act of *La Bohème*, what makes it a masterly piece of stage writing is the way the melodies are used — woven together, interrupted, connected by less noticeable but expertly contrived transitions, modulations, shifts of tempo and mood. His music for extremely dramatic moments — Tosca's spotting the knife with which to kill Scarpia, Minnie's cheating at cards — is often breathless and understated, calling no attention to itself *as music*, so that all eyes and anxieties will be focused on the stage. A great opera composer needs to know how to write all kinds of music for every situation — and when to write hardly any music at all.

Puccini, like every graduate of a conservatory, knew perfectly well how to put together a fugue, but the only time he even started to do so was in *Manon Lescaut*, Act II, when the lovers are getting ready to flee. ("Fuga" in Italian also means "flight.") This is a graphic use of a theoretical musical trick to illustrate an actual situation — bustling, tense, full of momentary activity that will quickly prove futile when the musical development, like the lover's escape, is abruptly cut short. Because he always made his technique subservient to the drama, Puccini drew heavy fire from scholarly types who wanted Italian music to aspire to high art. Following the lead of Giuseppe Martucci, a major conductor who venerated Schumann and Brahms and composed only symphonic or chamber music in emulation of them, these reformers hoped to pull Italian art out of the "gutter" of commercialism. But Puccini was perfectly happy, as Verdi had been, in the "gutter." For him it was a road to glory, and he saw no need to apologize for it. If he could have communicated with as many people, and done it as well, by writing symphonies and concertos, he might have

When Tito Ricordi took over his father's publishing firm, a bone of contention between him and Puccini was the rising career of Riccardo Zandonai (below), whom Tito considered his personal protégé, losing interest in Puccini. Modest and serious, Zandonai took his style from Wagner, Richard Strauss (bottom) and the French Impressionist composers; though his blend had less personality than Puccini's and his vocal line was less spontaneous, he proved a gifted colorist, and in his most famous work, Francesca da Rimini, *he vividly evoked the medieval past—something Puccini had been unable to do in* Edgar. *Strauss'* Salome *allured Puccini, but* Elektra, *more noisy and violent, he found repellent.*

Fantasy and humor leavened
Puccini's last opera, Turandot.
Below, the trio of maskers in Cecil
Beaton's 1961 Met production—
Robert Nagy (Pang), Charles
Anthony (Pong), Frank Guarrera
(Ping). Bottom, Franco Corelli and
Birgit Nilsson in the triumphant
finale of the same production—to
music completed by Franco Alfano.
Right, their predecessors Giacomo

Lauri-Volpi and Maria Jeritza,
who introduced Turandot to the
Met stage in November 1926. On
the opposite page, in a revival of
1974, Timur (James Morris) sings
his farewell to Liù (Teresa Zylis-
Gara) in the last music Puccini
lived to complete. Beneath, a card
inserted in the Met program the
evening of the day the composer died
—a day of international mourning.

written them too. But he knew the tortoise and the hare are two different creatures, and "Vive la différence!"

Though Puccini was one of a kind, his career bears comparison with that of one contemporary, Maurice Ravel. Both were charged with pandering to cheap tastes, manipulating audiences with a suspect technical expertise that exceeded their aesthetic judgment. Both went through hell in their work process, plagued by self-doubt, second thoughts and laborious perfectionism. And both suffered neuroses that fixed their attention on childhood emotions, particularly nostalgia for a warm, revered maternal figure, Goethe's "Eternal Feminine."

In Puccini's operas one sometimes has to feel that the characters are being tortured, psychologically and even physically — that their emotions, those flights of sad, impassioned melody, are being wrung out under pressure. Like all his dramatic devices, this one is used sparingly, so as not to wear out its effectiveness. But its very presence bothers some people a great deal, as it does in the operas of Benjamin Britten, and for the same reason: it reflects all too well the conflict and upheaval of our times, the decadent and morbid sensibility that invaded art as a result of all the cruelty in the world.

There is also in Puccini, however, as in Britten, the redeeming force of compassion. He depicts suffering, but his heart is with the sufferer. The composer in fact is baring his own soul, the inner torture of his life and music-making. It hurts, but it is human and real, not a fabrication for the purpose of getting a reaction. And amid the suffering there is beauty, the seductive, consoling beauty of Puccini's artful melodies.

Though intellectuals made a career of despising him, there is much to admire in Puccini's art. Stravinsky respected him, and Schoenberg was surprised by his courteous, genuine, intelligent concern for a younger colleague's innovations. He could set a stage as few others could, weaving together little details of locale and character, building up to the grand entrance of his heroine. His middle acts show a marshaling of dramatic forces to bring matters to a head. The last act sings of decline, a welling tide of despair at the perishability of human life and illusion. "Tear-jerkers" they may be, but Puccini's operas are among the finest of this genre: they use it without condescending, either to the genre or to the public. In his early maturity, Puccini was inevitably compared with the other verists — Giordano, Leoncavallo, Mascagni — all of whom were producing viable operas. Later, as his own style unfolded new petals, he was compared with Zandonai, Montemezzi, Respighi, Pizzetti, those of the up-and-coming generation. But as his fame increased, ultimately he was compared with himself. It was his own standard, the romance and intensity of his earlier triumphs, that he had to match. He confronted the challenge with honesty and humility. Unspoiled by success, he toiled conscientiously to help his talent grow. If he repeated himself, as in *Gianni Schicchi* and *La Rondine*, he did so knowingly, with a touch of wry humor. Within his boundaries, he wanted to explore — and to give the gift of love. Like his heroines, he died still reaching toward it, a love more vast than the ocean, one that would not die.

GIACOMO PUCCINI

BORN JUNE 23, 1858   DIED NOVEMBER 29, 1924

In Memoriam

Before the Fourth Act of tonight's performance of "La Boheme," the Orchestra, as a tribute, will play Chopin's Funeral March.

Few theater men can boast a reputation today to equal that of Puccini. What are the reasons behind this success? In the words of Giuseppe Adami, playwright, critic and librettist of later Puccini operas, "There was in him an extremely solid sense of conviction, an extremely firm will. He addressed himself to his art with tremendous ardor, because he was not lured away by the embrace of some momentary fascination: his credo consisted of a simplicity made all the clearer because it ran the risk of failing." Below, Puccini's writing desk at Torre del Lago with one of his manuscripts and the glasses he wore when working at the piano. Private and quiet in his lifetime, his studio is now a public shrine.

Between *Le Villi*, offered to the public in 1884, and *Turandot*, left unfinished in 1924, the cycle of Giacomo Puccini's artistic life was fulfilled—four decades in which his twelve operas were born in slow sequence, quite unlike the creative flow of the masters of the mid-nineteenth century, but showing by its very restraint the rigorous artistic conscience and problematic complexes underlying the Maestro's sense of musical theater. Music criticism today seems inclined to reconsider, to make amends for past disparagements. As for the public, its acceptance of Puccini's operas, enormous in his lifetime, seems to be continually growing and renewing. There is timeliness in the words of Filippo Sacchi, critic for *Il Corriere della Sera*, written the day after the Maestro's demise: "Puccini's was certainly the most universal artistic formula—not in the aesthetic but in the geographical sense—that Italy has produced since Verdi. There are so many countries in which our flag is not to be found, but Puccini is found everywhere . . . He spoke a language that everybody understood—the dialect of our feelings."

1858 - Giacomo Puccini born in Lucca on December 22, son of Michele, municipal orchestra leader, Cathedral organist, composer of operas and masses, and his wife, Albina Magi.

1876 - Writes *Symphonic Prelude*. Attends *Aida* in Pisa and returns deeply impressed.

1878 - Composes motet and Credo.

1880 - As exercise for Conservatory of Lucca, composes Mass for soloists and orchestra, incorporating motet and Credo of two years earlier. In autumn moves to Milan to enroll at local Conservatory, helped by study grant from Queen Margherita and loan from uncle. Has Bazzini and Ponchielli as teachers.

1883 - Completes studies at Conservatory, earning diploma with bronze medal. As senior thesis presents *Capriccio Sinfonico*, performed by student orchestra under Franco Faccio and later used for *La Bohème*.

1884 - Emerges on May 31 at Milan's Teatro Dal Verme with first opera, *Le Villi*, well received by press and public. Begins long relationship with publisher Giulio Ricordi. Puccini's mother dies; he falls in love and begins long affair with Elvira Bonturi, wife of a Luccan pharmacist, Gemignani.

1889 - After long gestation, Puccini's second opera, *Edgar*, goes onstage at La Scala on April 21, without lasting success.

1891 - Establishes himself at villa in Torre del Lago, near Lucca.

1893 - At Teatro Regio in Turin, reaps first big success with *Manon Lescaut*, February 1.

1896 - Again at Regio, again on February 1, the premiere of *La Bohème*, led by Arturo Toscanini. Better received by public than by critics, it is spur-

red on triumphal path by Palermo production under Leopoldo Mugnone.

1900 - Premiere of *Tosca* at Teatro Costanzi in Rome, January 14.

1904 - Finally marries Elvira after death of her first husband. February 17 marks premiere of *Madama Butterfly* at La Scala, fiasco redeemed by success of revised version at Brescia, May 28.

1907 - First trip to New York, where he sees Metropolitan Opera premieres of *Manon Lescaut* and *Butterfly*, Impressed by David Belasco's play *The Girl of the Golden West*.

1908 - Servant in Puccini household, Doria Manfredi, local Torre del Lago girl, commits suicide after jealous persecution by Elvira. Period of grave emotional stress for Puccini, with lawsuit against his wife by girl's family; marital relations strained to breaking point.

1910 - Second trip to New York, this time for triumphant world premiere of *La Fanciulla del West*, November 10, based on Belasco play with Toscanini conducting, Caruso, Emmy Destinn and Pasquale Amato in leading roles.

1912 - Death of Giulio Ricordi.

1917 - Puccini determines to make his mark on world of operetta. World War I changes plan: *La Rondine*, adapted into opera, makes debut at Casino Theatre in Monte Carlo, March 27.

1918 - Second Puccini world premiere at Metropolitan Opera —*Il Trittico*, trilogy of one-act operas on contrasting subjects, December 14.

1919 - Renato Simoni Proposes making opera of Carlo Gozzi's fantastic play *Turandot*.

1921 - Puccini settles down to work on *Turandot* at Viareggio, libretto by Adami and Simoni.

1924 - After treatment at Brussels clinic for throat cancer, Puccini dies of heart failure, November 29.

1926 - *Turandot* presented incomplete at La Scala under Toscanini, April 25. Subsequent performances include finale as completed by Franco Alfano from Puccini's sketches. Two months before his death, Puccini was given honorary title of senator. Now his remains are moved to Torre del Lago and reinterred in chapel of his villa.